THINK LIKE A STOIC

Also by Ken Mogi

The Little Book of Ikigai
The Way of Nagomi

THINK LIKE A STOIC

THE ANCIENT PATH TO A LIFE WELL LIVED

KEN MOGI

QUERCUS

First published in Great Britain in 2025 by Quercus
Part of John Murray Group

SRD

A CIP catalogue record for this book is available
from the British Library

HB ISBN 978 1 52943 581 8
EBOOK ISBN 978 1 52943 582 5

Typeset in Garamond by CC Book Production

Printed and bound in India by Manipal Technologies Limited, Manipal

MIX
Paper | Supporting
responsible forestry
FSC™ C104740

Papers used by Quercus are from well-managed forests and other responsible sources.

Quercus
Carmelite House
50 Victoria Embankment
London EC4Y 0DZ

John Murray Group
Part of Hodder & Stoughton Limited
An Hachette UK company

Dedicated to the first butterfly that I saw as a child.

Contents

Part One:
Stoicism and Everyday Life

Part Two:
Stoicism and the Future of Humans

Glossary

bushidō   The samurai code – the way of the warrior – priori-
tizing bravery, loyalty and self-sacrifice, sometimes
before life itself. Originating in the Kamakura period
(1192–1333), over time the martial code of *bushidō*
absorbed the influences of Confucianism and Buddhism. While *bushidō* also stresses the principles of
frugal living, kindness, honesty and personal honour,
the overriding emphasis is on duty, obligation and
honour. Ritual suicide, *seppuku*, also known as hara-
kiri, was institutionalized as a respected response to
dishonour or defeat. *Bushidō* remained a key ethos
in Japanese moral thinking right up to the end of the

Second World War; official instruction in the code was officially abandoned with Japan's defeat in 1945.

gaman   To endure with dignity. Seen as a very positive and desirable trait in Japan, *gaman* is both tolerating difficulty (often something unpleasant, painful or uncomfortable) without complaint, and also self-restraint – containing one's instinct to follow one's personal desires in order to support the wider group. Its achievement is seen as an expression of maturity.

ganbaru   Literally meaning 'best efforts', *ganbaru* is to do one's best and to persevere, even in tough times. When you experience adversity, *ganbaru* means you do not make excuses for failure but redouble your efforts.

giri   One's obligations and duty to the group; to serve one's superiors with a self-sacrificing devotion. Guided by a collective understanding of what is best for that person or group, *giri* is sense of loyalty that overrides personal wishes or opinions. Understanding others' *giri* is also a way of demonstrating consideration for them.

ikigai   One's personal purpose in life. Literally one's reason for getting up in the morning, *ikigai* can be both the small things that bring a person joy and a larger sense of purpose. Your *ikigai*, large or small, is a source of meaning that is not dependent on talent or worldly recognition.

kodawari   A personal sense of perfectionism. A commitment to a personal quality standard that involves paying attention to the smallest details and recognizing even tiny improvements.

nagomi   Balance, harmony. A concept that is deeply embedded in Japanese culture, *nagomi* expresses a sense of calm, comfort, and peace within oneself, and by extension, with the world around you. It might also mean accepting a certain balance of the good and bad in life, in order to sustain harmony within oneself and with the world at large.

nora   Literally meaning 'wild field', the word *nora*, added to a person or object, can be used to signify something stray, undomesticated, unauthorised or outside the rules.

ninjo   Human emotion or compassion – often a personal feeling that swells up in conflict with one's *giri*, or sense of duty.

zatsudan Literally meaning 'miscellaneous talks', this is the wide-ranging informal social exchanges that bind Japanese society together.

Preface

This is a book that sets out to offer some help with the challenges of modern life. Within these pages, I will do my best to offer a vision to my readers – across the spectrum of humanity, from ordinary people to (would-be) leaders, extrovert to introvert, ambitious to humble, hungry to satisfied, if not quite perhaps from slave to emperor – a vision of how the ancient wisdom of Stoicism might help us navigate a confusing and overwhelming age.

In the process, I will go through a wide range of subjects, including everyday life issues such as managing our emotions, accepting ourselves, social communication, how to face others, how to deal with life's uncertainties, happiness, etc., on the one hand, and fundamental and difficult issues such as creativity, consciousness, free will, infinity and the universe, Earth's environment and the future of human civilization on the other. By the time you finish reading this book, you will be convinced that these big issues do have a relevance to the seemingly small problems of your private life. In addition, I will introduce a mega-star from ancient Greece viewed under a new spotlight and discuss the possibility that the world we live in – no matter how broken it might seem – is actually the best of all possible worlds.

I am a neuroscientist, writer and broadcaster based in Tokyo, Japan, and the author of books such as *The Little Book of Ikigai* and *The Way of Nagomi*. My book on *ikigai* (one's personal reason for living) has been published in 32 languages and 58 countries, and became a bestseller in Germany after it appeared in a popular TV detective drama. It was actually the number-one non-fiction bestseller there in 2024. This is my first international title that is not just about Japan, though my Japanese perspective will very likely shine through.

Stoicism is not specific to a culture, nor is it an ideology. It is a philosophy of life, one that constantly evolves and adapts to the changing times.

Let's explore it together.

Introduction

It used to be that this was a world of scarcity. Our ancestors, right back to the microorganisms that preceded us hundreds of millions of years ago, had to fight for their survival, searching for things to eat and looking for places where they could safely hide. Times have changed. Now we are living in a world of abundance, at least for the more fortunate among us. This applies not only to material wealth, but also, and particularly, to informational abundance. At the same time, some of us may be feeling eerily empty in soul, even on the verge of burnout, lost in the great ocean of life, which sometimes appears to be senseless and cruel. Perhaps that is why you have picked up and are now reading this book.

One crucial factor in this emptiness is the disappearance of traditional values and modes of thinking. For many people in the world, it is no longer the case that one can just follow pre-fixed ideas and norms to lead a satisfying life in the spiritual sense. It is not that we are less human than our ancestors. We may actually be more so, but we are human in so many different ways, with inputs from many cultures. We have diversity rather than monoculture, which is wonderful, but sometimes overwhelming.

We are living in an era where it is becoming increasingly difficult to make appropriate choices for ourselves. In 1970, the futurist Alvin Toffler predicted a condition he called 'choice overload'. In the Information Age, as he called it, we would be faced with the prospect of having to choose from a multitude of alternatives presented either virtually or physically, increasingly more of the former, even before the age of the metaverse kicked in. This age has now arrived. A teenager quickly flipping through the offerings from TikTok, Instagram or YouTube is performing an exercise both specific to our time, and one predicted by Toffler several decades ago. With the flood of content generated by artificial intelligence, 'choice overload' will only become even more overwhelming in the coming years.

The problem is not just too much information. Modern life is complex, and our lives are branching out in so many directions. It is literally everything everywhere all at once, even for the most ordinary among us. And even if we make the best decision at an important crossroad, there is no guarantee that the results will be great, or even benign, because of 'dynamical chaos', as the meteorologist Edward Lorenz termed it in the 1970s. Complex systems display great unpredictability – even small differences in the initial state can lead to quite unexpectedly large differences in outcome. This is the famous butterfly effect, which suggests that a butterfly flapping its wings in the tropical rainforest of the Amazon could eventually determine whether a tornado develops in, say, Texas, USA. The astonishing thing is that this is not a mere metaphor but a mathematical truth in the most rigorous sense.

The reality of the butterfly effect in our lives is that there is no such thing as a distinction between grave and trivial choices. Which college you go to, what occupation you choose for yourself, where you live, whom you marry – we recognize these things as important decisions in life. But if you take chaos theory at face value, choosing what you have for lunch today or what clothes you wear, or whether you take a right turn or a left at the next junction could potentially lead to enormous differences in how your life turns out. The world is a chaotic place and there is no way to know if a particular choice is optimal or not, no matter how clever and informed you may be or how hard you may try.

Today, dynamical chaos and information overload are flanked by the uncertainties of globalization, environmental change and artificial intelligence. With seemingly intractable problems such as global warming, fake news and political echo chambers, living is becoming increasingly challenging. And still, in our private lives, we have the same old problems concerning family, friends, career choices and how to make ends meet. We clearly need a vision and guidance. But how can we find them, in this liberal but unnerving void of pre-fixed values? Is there an enlightened way to proceed from here?

I propose that, in this age, we need to study in earnest and perhaps make our own a particular philosophical tradition: Stoicism.

Stoicism dates back to ancient Greece. The Stoic school as we know it today was started by Zeno of Citium (*c.* 334 BC–*c.* 262 BC). The name 'Stoic' comes from the word *stoa*, or painted porch – the place where Zeno taught his ideas in ancient Athens. As a young man, Zeno experienced and survived a shipwreck. Later, in a bookshop in Athens, he came upon a description of Socrates in *Memorabilia* by Xenophon (a disciple of Socrates). Impressed by Xenophon's depiction, Zeno became interested in philosophy. This was the beginning of his philosophical investigations, which eventually led to the founding of the Stoic school.

Thus, in an indirect but quite essential and spiritual way, Socrates could be considered the father of Stoicism. Indeed, many scholars identify Socrates as one of the important thinkers of Stoicism, and many Stoic writers – Zeno, Seneca, Marcus Aurelius and Epictetus among them – have found inspiration and guidance in his life and teaching.

For example, throughout his life, Socrates strived to live

in harmony with reason and nature. Socrates knew how to engage in open dialogue and learn from other people. He was also tolerant of others' peculiarities, being well aware of his own ignorance. Finally, Socrates faced his own death with resignation. Many of these traits are the foundation for the Stoic way of life, and this Socratic association gives depth and resonance to the Stoic ethos, a theme we will come back to later in this book.

The Stoic school remained popular for more than 500 years and the works of later Stoic writers such as Seneca, in the first century BCE, Epictetus, the former slave, and Marcus Aurelius, the Roman emperor from 160–180 CE offer us great pillars of wisdom to reference. But can such an ancient wisdom serve the modern man in any way beyond the context of a liberal-arts curriculum?

Indeed it can. There is nothing new under the sun. In fact, as far as a philosophy of life goes, there might not be much to add to what has been already written in the Stoicism canon. The essential messages of Stoicism remain relevant, because we are all still human, and the essence of our existence has not changed so much over the years. We still dream, love, sometimes get disappointed, in Stoic ways. Isn't that wonderful?

And yet, I do feel that there is a pressing need to update how we approach Stoicism to reflect the parameters of the modern day, and the practical and psychological needs of people now.

One advantage of our time is that we humans have more knowledge about ourselves and the world around us than the Stoic greats had access to. A modern interpretation and extension of Stoicism might draw on fields such as neuroscience, cognitive science, psychology, network science, economics and artificial intelligence. Insights from physics and cosmology are also surprisingly relevant. In particular, those from neuroscience tell us how we adapt to the changing environment of modern times by absorbing and interpreting sensory data from outside and taking appropriate actions, thus affecting the plasticity of neural networks in the brain. In this process, understanding and implementing concepts that describe our attitudes towards the world become crucial. Grasping an updated version of Stoicism and making it one's own is part of this.

For example, one of the most important themes of Socrates' teaching, and the Stoic school, was the concept of alignment. The Stoics regarded humans as part of the universe, subject to natural laws. Their belief was that our individual natures were all part of universal nature and that our job as humans was to accept the world as it is and live in a manner that corresponds to it. Or, as Marcus Aurelius said (*Meditations* 6, XLIX), 'That which is not good for the beehive cannot be good for the bee'.

In the present day, 'alignment' has further, yet interestingly related, meanings. In neuroscience, alignment is the result of the human brain's learning process, the outcome of making sensory inputs and actions that are consistent with each other. In artificial intelligence, 'alignment' is used as a concept to lead research and development, as in 'AI alignment'. An essential aspect of alignment in the AI sense is that the aligned entities (such as humans and AIs) each retain their individual existence, agency and traits, and are not necessarily merged and made into one. While they keep their separate identities, alignment allows the entities to be in harmony with each other (or as we Japanese would say, in a state of *nagomi*), so that the system as a whole can function in a robust and sustainable manner. The alignments between humans and artificial intelligence, humans and nature, and among people of different and unique characters is going to be vitally important in our modern world. In this respect, Stoicism can show how each one of us can live as an individual, apart from but in tune with the grand designs of the universe.

So, in this book, I would like to add insights particular to our present time, humbly, if I may. I will try to provide a wide spectrum of viewpoints, from those which help the reader's everyday life to those which have profound implications for our very existence as human beings. One of the ultimate goals of the great Stoic thinkers and the people who followed their writings was to find peace amid the turmoil of the world and attain solace for the soul. Without understanding who we really are, we cannot find solace for the soul, even in the context of everyday life. As the title of Seneca's great work suggests, I would like to provide 'Consolations' to the reader.

From its origin in Greek and Roman times to the present day,

Stoicism is a school of thought that springs from the Western world and, consequently, has strong Western connotations. However, it is important to realize that Stoicism as it stands today, and as it might be used in the future, is a rewardingly multicultural ethos.

All over the world, people practise folk stoicism (that is stoicism as a way of life rather than a philosophical concept) in their own ways, without knowing the theoretical, historical or scientific basis for it. Every ordinary person can be a Stoic. An athlete, an artist, a businessperson, a mother, a father, a child, an old person can be a Stoic. Some people explicitly describe themselves as stoic; others are stoic without being aware that they are. Some have never come across the concept, but practise it all the same, especially in regions where the influence of the Western canon has not reached. In all cases, people are stoic as they go about the business of life because they've got to be. Stoicism, as I argue in this book, is an essential attitude to life.

The ethics and codes of behaviour that resonate with Stoicism can be found across many different cultures. In the tradition of Chinese philosophy, parallels can be found in the thinking of *Tao*, in which humans are encouraged to follow the orders of nature, rather than resist them. Many people regard the traditional *haka* dance of the indigenous Maori people in New Zealand as an expression of the Stoic spirit. In Africa, the philosophy of life of the Maasai people in Kenya and Tanzania shows wonderful interpretations of Stoic thinking. Some may argue that the spiritual values expressed in such Hollywood franchises as *Star Wars* and *Karate Kid* are Stoic in their essence, influenced by many different cultural origins. And I am quite certain that the music and dance of Taylor Swift are Stoic, especially having been lucky enough to enjoy her Eras tour in Tokyo Dome, performed with astonishing skill and determination. Indeed, Stoicism today is a global phenomenon, as it should be, when you consider its central importance to how we live.

In my native Japan, the concept of Stoicism only arrived as an explicit idea during the process of modernization, which started with the Meiji Restoration of 1868, kick-starting a rapid restructuring of the nation under imperial rule. As such, it is relatively new. However, if you look back through Japanese history, you will find that something equivalent to

Stoicism has been always there, so that the Japanese people have known it, in a very embodied and robust way, over hundreds of years. Confucianism, which emphasized social harmony, has certainly influenced the 'stoic' way the Japanese restrain themselves, especially in social contexts involving different age groups, while the concept of *gaman* – expressing the idea of enduring difficulty with dignity – is a ubiquitous Japanese one that describes various ways to contain one's actions and speech, so as not to go beyond what is socially acceptable. *Gaman* has been influenced by Confucianism in part but remains distinctively Japanese, especially in the Zen Buddhist context. *Gaman* most likely originated from the original living conditions in Japan, where the demands of rice farming in our mountainous nation meant people had to find ways to co-exist harmoniously. Even nowadays, *gaman* is still apparent in every aspect of Japanese society. A mother will quite typically preach it to her child, especially in a situation where the eyes of the others are there to witness the child's behaviour. *Gaman* is also the protocol for the majority of employees, who tend to work long hours without complaining. Shinto, as the indigenous Japanese religion, has also been pivotal in the formation of the Japanese character, especially as regards the purity and serenity of mind emphasized in samurai ethics.

Growing up in Japan, I could not help but be influenced by these elements. Then, when I was ten or so, I started to read Western literature quite extensively, as is usually the case for kids with academic interests in post-modernization Japan, and first encountered the Greek philosophers, including Socrates. As a teenager, I read Marcus Aurelius and other Stoic writers, too. If it was not evident to me then how these Stoic canons related to the Japanese way of life, I see the parallels between the different cultural heritages now. For example, is there any link between the samurai ethic of *bushidō*, which prioritized service to the master and community over one's own interests, even to the point of sacrificing one's own life if necessary, and the philosophy of Socrates, who accepted his own death without much fuss? Or how about Albert Einstein, who once said that he would simply lie down and wait for the time when the last day of his life came? Are Socrates and Einstein both samurais in the Stoic spirit? Such considerations, I think, are useful as a way of putting ideas and thoughts related to Stoicism in a historical and cultural perspective in the global village today, beyond national borders.

There are great writers who are Stoics without explicitly professing it: Leo Tolstoy, Marcel Proust, Virginia Woolf, Ernest Hemingway and Kazuo Ishiguro, to name but a few. Ishiguro's character Stevens, the dutiful butler in his epic novel *The Remains of the Day*, would seem to many the epitome of Stoicism – soldiering on with a 'stiff upper lip'. But it seems to me that the Stoicism expressed here is multicultural in its very nature. Although the portrayed society and human behaviour are obviously British, the author, having immigrated from Japan to the UK at the age of five, has brought something of the Japanese version of Stoicism into the novel, most notably elements from the traditions of Zen Buddhism and samurai ethics. When Stevens is caught between the desire to attend his father's dying moments and the requirement to perform his duty as a butler at an important dinner in the great house, he demonstrates a very Japanese version of Stoicism, in which one is encouraged to restrain one's emotions or *ninjo* (a Japanese word literally meaning 'human emotion', which is regarded as the bonding principle in Japan) in order to play one's part in the group. Showing *giri* (another Japanese word, meaning 'obligations') is an alignment that was part of the cooperation required for rice farming, but also remains a key way of behaving in Japan today. It was Ishiguro's genius to write a story of such pure Englishness while the undertone of Stoicism was essentially multicultural.

Perhaps Stoicism is adaptable across cultures and ages because it is not perceived to have a charismatic figure as such, from whom a whole principle stems. In fact, Stoicism started from a negation of a *cult of personality* (more on this later). Although certain individuals played a pivotal role in defining what Stoicism is, it never became a movement under a particular person's name. Stoicism is rather a collective and open-ended discipline, ready to be worked on and improved by everybody. In other words, Stoicism is about all of us.

Nor is Stoicism about a particular tradition described by a particular proper noun. It is about generic ways in which humans have been living, currently live and, with a little bit of luck, will keep living for many centuries to come. Stoicism

shows us a way that the human brain can cope, become resilient and even exhibit creativity in times of great uncertainty
and difficulty. And that has never been more necessary than
now.

As I begin the appraisal of Stoicism in the modern context,
I would like to offer you ten statements towards a working
definition of what Stoicism might be for us in the modern
world. These are not exhaustive or mutually independent
but they might be something to ponder as you read this
book.

1. Stoicism is about how one streamlines one's resources
   and efforts as one goes through the uncertainties of
   life.
2. Stoicism is a way of making one's best effort under
   any circumstances.
3. Stoicism is a process by which one reappraises one's
   emotions to arrive at a positive and proactive view
   of life.
4. Stoicism is maintaining a balance of the self, body

and personal agency while interacting in a complex and unpredictable environment.

5. Stoicism is coming to terms with one's own unique characteristics and traits, accepting oneself and nurturing self-love.

6. Stoicism is becoming liberated from life's proxy goals and navigating towards the heart's true desires.

7. Stoicism is aligning one's life with one's inner voices, and the laws of the world.

8. Stoicism is about seeing things clearly, knowing one's own limitations, while having a sense of wonder for the unknown and dreaming of one's eventual possibilities.

9. Stoicism is about appreciating and celebrating the diversity within oneself and in the universe.

10. Stoicism is about keeping one's personal integrity under any circumstances, so as to see clearly the shape of one's soul.

By the time you finish reading this book, the above statements will hopefully make sense to you in rewarding and profound ways. At the same time, I hope that exploring the Stoic way will leave you better prepared for the challenges of the present day, with a more optimistic outlook for the future.

To be optimistic is to be Stoic. And to be optimistic is human.

Indeed, to be Stoic is human.

So let us start our journey into the heart of Stoicism.

PART ONE:

Stoicism and Everyday Life

CHAPTER 1

What do we mean when we call someone stoic?

I once met an extraordinary gentleman on a luxury cruise ship. I was on board to give public lectures. That gentleman, whom I call by the code name Mr Four Seasons, apparently came from a very privileged background. His story was incredible. Originally from western Japan, he spent eleven months of every year abroad, staying in places like Europe, Australia, Hawaii, etc. He had houses here and there. Mr Four Seasons was a gentle, exquisite person, wearing a colourful and elegantly designed shirt, and accompanied by an equally elegant lady wife. I happened to share a dinner table with the couple. Mr Four Seasons had just turned eighty.

I did not ask what he used to do for his living. He might have been involved in some very important jobs, but it was also apparent that he did not have to work for a living.

He told me that he had taken the world cruise for ten years in a row. He said that, when he was on the cruise ship, he would get up at four every morning and go to the ship's gym to run on the treadmill machine. On a good day, he would run at 15km/hour. He ran twice a day, two hours each time. Although the luxury cruise ship offered many entertainments, Mr Four Seasons never went to the theatre, as his lady wife did. Every day, he just went to the gym to run. His dream was to win in the World Masters Athletics competition at the age of one hundred, he said. He also kept detailed diaries on the cruise and his other adventures in the world, which, by the time I met him, amounted to thirty-seven notebooks. I do not believe he has any plans to publish them.

The image of this extremely wealthy gentleman running for several hours every day on a luxury cruise ship left a vivid, lasting impression on me. Presumably, Mr Four Seasons had the means to enjoy almost any pleasure life had to offer. Every year he enjoyed a trip on a cruise ship where everything was prepared for him and his lady wife in the most refined manner. However, for some unknown reason, Mr Four Seasons chose a very Stoic way of life for himself.

I met Mr and Mrs Four Seasons on my way from New York to Costa Rica. By the time I joined, the world cruise was about two-thirds over, having gone through Yokohama, Kobe, Singapore, the Maldives, South Africa, Spain, Germany and the UK. On the evening I met him, Mr Four Seasons was enjoying a bottle of red wine: he was celebrating the mid-journey point amid his arduous training days, he said. Up until the ship reached New York, he had not had a drop. 'I am going to get up at four o'clock tomorrow and run,' was his last remark, as the good couple retired for the night.

For some strange reason, although we did not discuss Stoicism, Mr Four Seasons reminded me of Marcus Aurelius and other privileged people over the course of human history, who, in the midst of material abundance, chose to live a Stoic life. For these people, careful recruitment of their resources and execution of their attention, accompanied by intelligent assignments of sensory pleasures, exploration and arduous physical exercises are the way of choice. There is something essentially human about a life lived this way. It is as if Stoicism is the only way to make sense of one's existence in this whirlpool of material abundance we call the universe.

When you observe human behaviour, one of the hallmarks of a person's nature is how she or he behaves when they become successful and/or famous. In Japan, where the experience of collaborating in situations such as the rice field has nurtured a culture of humility, there is a saying 'a rice ear hangs its head low as it ripens', which is an observation of what actually happens to rice, as well as a metaphor for how you should behave in success. As I discussed in my book *The Way of Nagomi*, in Japan rice is considered to represent desirable qualities in nature and humans. Unfortunately, not all people are like rice. There are those who remain modest as they succeed – they tend to be OK, with a moderate lifestyle. Then there are others who let success go to their heads, and become arrogant, less respectful, extravagant, and lead unsustainable lifestyles. In the end, they might find themselves in great trouble.

In this respect, it is interesting to note that the Stoic Marcus Aurelius reacted to the increasing pomp and circumstances of his life as heir apparent to the Imperial throne with subdued resignation. It cannot be said that he enjoyed being the emperor of the Roman Empire, yet there is something about the way he took his prestige and fame that is genuinely symbolic of what Stoicism represents. His humility meant he could think in terms of conditions common to all people and ponder universal human problems that occur whether one is the Emperor of the Roman Empire or a slave. Humility is one of the hallmarks of Stoicism.

In a sense, every one of us faces a challenge similar to Mr Four Seasons in modern life, albeit not necessarily on such a grand scale as on a luxury cruise ship. Increasingly, life in developed nations is characterized by material and informational abundance at a reduced cost. In Japan, where I live, many young people seem to be content to migrate between school, part-time jobs (which are called *arubaito*, a loanword after the German *arbeit*) and convenience stores (called *konbini* in modern Japanese). Indeed, Japanese *konbini* are world famous for providing all sorts of foods, daily items, basic clothing and even electronics. Young people in Japan are blessed with material sufficiency from the convenience store and informational abundance from social media and game consoles.

But as advancements in technology make modern life increasingly comfortable, we need wisdom to help us restrain ourselves. We need to tolerate challenge and discomfort from time to time to maintain the balance of mind and body, just as Mr Four Seasons did on the luxury cruise ship. In this pursuit, insights from the Stoic canon can be useful. In the midst of plenty Marcus Aurelius was rather like Mr Four Seasons, restraining himself from indulging too much in the pleasures available and making sure to do things that were good for his body and mind.

So, what do we mean when we call someone 'Stoic'? If a person can be humble, no matter their fortune, we might say they are stoic. Socrates certainly knew how to remain humble and reserved, treating people around him with respect. If a person knows how to restrain themselves amid material comfort and informational abundance, we can recognize a

Stoic there. In the modern world, everyone can aspire to be a Stoic; we can have fruitful lives like a ripening rice ear, and yet make ourselves harmonious and sustainable by lowering our heads. That is the Stoic way, open to all of us.

CHAPTER 2

Can you control it?

In the intricate and vast web of modern life, there are certain things that we can hope to control, and certain things we simply cannot, no matter how hard we may try. The Stoic greats Epictetus and Marcus Aurelius both wrote about the issue of controllability in life, believing it to be a central and crucially important issue. Epictetus made the distinction between the controllable (*prohairetic*) and uncontrollable (*aprohairetic*) as the foundation for his philosophy. Marcus Aurelius wrote about the futility of trying to affect things out of one's control. Given the complexity of the Roman Empire, it would have been difficult for Marcus Aurelius to control every state affair, even if, as emperor, that was precisely his job description. You might think that life becomes more controllable as you climb the social ladder, but they show that this principle of Stoicism applies to people from all social positions, whether a slave (Epictetus) or an emperor (Marcus Aurelius).

The difficulty of controlling things is a problem for us all today. The illusion of controllability often leads to stress and unbalanced, or misaligned, behaviour. For example, when you love someone, you may wish to have your love returned. But believing that you can expect, let alone control the affections of another by your own efforts, without their consent, could end up with you becoming a stalker. As a parent, you may want your child to grow and develop in certain ways and direct your parental efforts accordingly, but if you try to control your child unreasonably, that could simply turn into abuse. If you are a fan of a football club, it is fun to root for that team in a match. But if you are under the illusion that your cheers can control the results, statistically you will be disappointed and unhappy about fifty per cent of the time.

Modern life is full of pitfalls in which we might suffer from an illusory sense of control. Trying to solve what mathematicians call 'ill-posed problems' – problems with no stable solution due to an inappropriate approach – can cause a lot of stress, to the detriment of our health and well-being. So, one might say, try to avoid the illusion that you can control something that you simply cannot. Simple. End of story.

Well, not so fast. When you get to grips with this issue, you realize that you cannot start from the assumption that it is easy to make out the border between the controllable and uncontrollable. Furthermore, even when you can make the distinction, it is not always the case that the two can be clearly separated.

Stoicism is first and foremost about making an educated triage of what is controllable and what is not. You do your best with those things you can control. Things you cannot control, you leave to random outcomes, or, as the contemporaries of Marcus Aurelius would have phrased it, fate.

The adjective *educated* is essential here. Babies and small children do not understand the divide. That is why they are often distressed and cry, sometimes for the moon. Indeed, it is through experiencing disillusionment and disappointment that children eventually learn what is controllable and what is not. And as we grow, we accumulate knowledge and skills and develop our ability to discern things. We become better at making an *educated* distinction between what is by its nature controllable and what is not, though the border might be different from person to person. Maturity means being increasingly accurate in this differentiation, and Stoicism means knowing that difference.

In Japan, *gaman*, the ability to endure with patience, is founded on making this distinction – the understanding that one's own behaviour is under one's own control. In fact, *gaman*, especially in children, is seen as a mark of maturity. In modern life, as the range of things we interact with has expanded, it is particularly crucial to realize what lies beyond our control. Even grown-up adults, when dealing with the unfamiliar and unknown world of globalization and artificial intelligence, find it difficult to distinguish the controllable from the uncontrollable.

The good news is that as humans, the fact that we have bodies gives us a huge advantage in making the triage of controllability. In the human brain, we perceive our own bodies to be something controllable, but this is a skill we have acquired. When a baby is born, it does not know where its body begins and ends. In exploring itself and the world around it, the baby touches things, and in that process discovers the border between the self and non-self. When you touch your own body, there are simultaneous sensations of touching and being touched, a process called self-touch. When you touch somebody else, there is only a sense of touching. When you are touched by someone, there is only a sense of being touched. Thus, through the distinctions between sensations of touching, being touched and self-touch, we learn the border between the self and non-self. Later, this will form the cognitive foundation for communication. A striking example is tickling. It is well known that you cannot tickle yourself. In the brain, information about your motor activities (tickling) is sent to the sensory areas, so that when you self-tickle, the sensory information is cancelled out. In order to feel ticklish, you need someone else to do the tickling. In addition, you need to be in an intimate relationship with that someone to feel ticklish. Otherwise, it won't feel ticklish at all. For example, if a stranger approaches you and tickles you, it is frightening rather than ticklish. So, the seemingly simple sensation of feeling ticklish is the result of a complex series of information processing in the brain regarding the body, the self and the non-self, and the bodily and social boundaries.

Once the brain knows the physical bodily border, the default assumption would be that one is able to control one's body. Indeed, as we grow and develop, we *are* better able to control and move our bodies. A baby starts by crawling, then stands on feet clumsily, and eventually walks, runs and even dances. This is an incredible achievement on the part of the brain circuits involved, such as the motor, premotor and supplementary motor cortices, as well as other brain areas such as the basal ganglia and the cerebellum.

However, as all of us know, it is not always the case that we can control our bodies at will. Anybody who has tried to do well in swimming, tennis, golf, baseball or any other sport knows how difficult it can sometimes be to move one's body exactly as intended. On another, more fundamental level, some of our bodily functions are still outside our conscious control. For example, the movements and functions of the bowel. (Increasingly, researchers are finding out more about the intricate functional connectivity between the brain and gut, which work in a framework called the brain–gut axis. In order for the brain to function well, one needs to have a balanced colony of gut microbiome; the function of the gut, in turn, sometimes critically depends on the balanced functioning of the mind–brain. So, to have a healthy brain life, you need a healthy gut life, and vice versa; your brain and gut need to work as a team. In other words, your conscious and unconscious need to tango.)

We humans have a unique position among animals in that we can make and use various tools. The German–American historian and philosopher Hannah Arendt and the French philosopher Henri Bergson stressed the importance of thinking of humans as *Homo Faber* (Man the Maker). Tools are crucially important for human life, and the human brain treats them as integral parts of our human existence. In fact, measurements of brain activity have shown that when we use tools, our neural circuits regard them as extended bodies. For example, when we use a rake to draw items closer to the body, the brain represents the rake as an extension of the arm and hand. When we drive a car, it is represented in the brain as an extended body, so that we may be able to manoeuvre it as if it *was* our own body (more on this in the next chapter).

As we have made progress in civilization, the extended body has become ever more sophisticated. The epic scene in Stanley Kubrick's film *2001: A Space Odyssey*, in which a primordial man throws a bone into the air which turns into a spaceship, beautifully illustrates the way our bodily extension has expanded over the years, from simple tools to sophisticated machinery such as cars, trains, planes and even spaceships.

Our extended-body image is important as it supports our sense of agency. As conscious beings with the illusion of free will, we feel ourselves to be agents, and the body represents the domain of our direct agency (except for uncontrollable parts, such as the gut). As the body image is extended via the tools we use, so our sense of agency is also enlarged.

This bookkeeping of one's agency constitutes the very foundation of the Stoic way of life. Unless you know the bounds of your body, and the extent to which you can control it, you cannot carry out a triage of what is controllable and what is not. Confusion about one's agency can lead to a total disruption of Stoicism.

The extended-body metaphor can also be applied to tools such as the mobile phone, tablet or laptop computer and to the cyber and informational spheres. The extended body consists not only of physical tools but also information systems. Today, when we use the internet, we feel we have agency over the copies of the self that represent us on our social media accounts, such as X (formerly known as Twitter), Instagram and TikTok. When we put information out into the world through these media, we feel as if the cyber or informational copies of us are virtual agents trying to influence things far beyond our physical reach. When we post on X, we are hoping, perhaps, to spread messages or images that are favourable about ourselves. If our post is reposted one thousand times, and receives a million likes, it might feel as if our virtual presence has been magnified that many times. But as anyone who has attempted public relations using these platforms will acknowledge, it is tremendously difficult to control the effects of our social media output. It is like walking a tightrope, where a heart-warming story sits too close to devastating bad press, separated only by the breadth of a hair.

So our existence on social media creates a fundamentally confusing situation when it comes to the bookkeeping of our agency. When you are dealing with your physical body, you know, more or less, what is going to happen. When you pick up an apple, it will stay in your hand, unless you eat it or throw it away. Not so for your extended self on social media. You don't really know what is going to happen. Indeed, some advise steering clear of social media activities altogether for fear of the uncertainties involved, from inciting trolls to inviting gross misinterpretations.

The perception of our cyber and informational selves as part of the extended body brings even mature adults back to lessons they learned as babies in Body Control 101. Babies learn to distinguish the bodily self and non-self through trial and error. The challenge for the modern human is to learn where their extended body starts and ends and sort out the uncertainties involved, grasping which bits are under their control. It is also interesting to note here that the problems of the body and agency are interwoven with the relationship between the self and others. In other words, how to communicate and deal with other people. Here, the Japanese way of seeking a *nagomi* relationship with others, through an ethos such as *gaman*, provides a useful model.

Many texts by Stoics such as Seneca, Epictetus and Marcus Aurelius which are concerned with what we can control ask what we might expect of other people. Stoic writers repeatedly state that it is futile to expect things from others, let alone depend on their goodwill for one's happiness. This particular tenet of Stoicism is based on a realistic perception of what life entails. For example, if you are kind to a person, there is no guarantee you will be treated in the same spirit. Obviously, it might seem that if you have been treated kindly, it would be ethical to be kind to that person in return, but Stoicism is not about ethics as such. Stoicism is larger than ethics. It is a way to align oneself even with an unethical world, while, of course, not being unethical yourself. In a nutshell, Stoicism is about how to live in the world as it is, not as you would like it to be.

When you think about your friends and family, you know that you cannot always rely on their consistent responses in your favour. You cannot expect people around you to be reasonable; in fact, it is not reasonable to expect people around you to be reasonable. A moral person might expect others to behave in ethical ways, because they try to be ethical themselves. A Stoic does not start from such an assumption. A Stoic does not expect others to be ethical, although that would be certainly desirable. Sure, in an ideal world, all people would be ethical, reasonable and kind, but demanding an ideal world has its own philosophical pitfalls, as we will get on to later.

The first step of becoming a Stoic, then, is never to expect a certain behaviour from anyone. That way you will never be disappointed, because you do not expect good things from others to begin with. If someone is kind to you or even loves you, that is really great and rewarding, but when someone does not treat you kindly, that is OK, too, because that's the way it is. It is not even an ethical issue. It is about a *scientific* understanding of the controllability of the world around you. Other people, no matter how dear to you, are not controllable, because they do not constitute your own body or agency. The world is not your body, you cannot control it, and Stoicism is not about ethics.

So, in a world becoming increasingly complex and incomprehensible, how might we make a distinction between controllable and uncontrollable things? As we have seen in this chapter, a good rule of the thumb, deeply rooted in the neurophysiology of the brain, is to fall back on one's own body image. Whenever you are dealing with a new social context, or a novel technology, ask yourself how you feel in terms of your body. Does it feel intact, or disrupted? How is your body extended? When you are in a team, do you feel physically one with other team members? When you are using a new technological tool such as generative AIs, how does your body feel in relation to that?

Just like a newborn child explores its own body in search of the border between the self and non-self, and the potentials and limits of agency, we humans are in a constant process of updating our relationships with the world. In that process, our bodies are extended, checked, updated, questioned and then reassessed. Stoicism is an embodied approach to life, and we dance in the modern world with our extended bodies, to the Stoic music.

CHAPTER 3

Coming to terms with emotions

Humans are social animals. Yet it is interesting to note that most of the things that are uncontrollable to us are those associated with other people. For example, how others think and feel are matters that we cannot control. Their personalities are outside the bounds of what we can control. Their abilities are things we cannot directly improve upon, except through the long and arduous process we call education.

On social media, we constantly see people rubbishing others, calling each other fools. It may be the case that, in one's view, other people on social media are of inferior intellectual calibre. It is not, however, stoic to rant on about their stupidity. There is no controlling someone else's stupidity anyway, so it will not help. I am not saying here that giving vent to one's emotions is necessarily a bad thing. It may be that doing so could serve some personal or social purpose. However, we do need to put our emotional expression into context, so that we can make our emotions robust, in alignment with our relationship with others, and start living a Stoic life.

There is a popular misinterpretation and misrepresentation of Stoicism in which a stoic person is assumed to be someone who is devoid of emotions. This idea might have originated through our encounters with people we don't understand well, as it is easier to depict a stranger as emotionless, rather than trying to come to an understanding. Actually, no person is an island, disconnected from the continent of emotions. Far from it. In Kazuo Ishiguro's *The Remains of the Day* the butler, Stevens, might appear to be an emotionless manservant before his master, but he is actually capable of very human emotions, especially towards his colleague Miss Kenton at Darlington Hall. Out of respect for his opponent, a Japanese sumo wrestler will not express any emotion, even if he wins in an important bout, but inside he will be full of joy, evidenced by his red eyes and occasional shedding of tears. And if you read the *Meditations* of Marcus Aurelius, you will see that the emperor as an individual had tremendously nuanced emotions about himself and those around him. In fact, you *need* to be a person with a full spectrum of rich emotions – ups and downs, moved and moving, hilarious and sombre, joyous and sorrowful – if you are to deal with life in a robust and stoic way.

Humans have a range of emotions, some positive, others negative. In response to adversarial events, the brain's emotional circuits, with the amygdala at the hub, generate emotions such as anger, jealousy and anxiety. And, as all of us know too well, when these emotions take hold there's not much we can do that will be constructive. Indeed, if we do act based on these emotions, the outcome will likely be negative, perhaps even devastating.

Many Stoic writers have written about the importance of coming to terms with emotions, especially powerful ones such as anger. Seneca, for instance, discusses anger at length, judging it to be useless and futile, and even says that it has done more damage to humans than plague. It is crucial to realize that you cannot really control the emotions you have, especially in terms of suppression. People often say that you should not get angry, that anger typically brings only disastrous consequences, both to those who become angry, and to those exposed to the wrath. However, to say 'you should not get angry' is not really practical, not only in terms of the social implications or also in view of neurophysiology. You *do* sometimes get angry. Emotions just happen, and all you can do is to interpret and handle them in an intelligent and creative manner. So, the question is how to curb your anger (as well as your enthusiasm). Here, it is important to note that the value of emotions is not binary – positive or negative. Emotions generally taken to be negative could be turned towards positive effects in life if you know how to interpret and handle them in an intelligent way. Anger, for example, could be turned into fuel for change.

So, the issue is not how to suppress emotions, but how to come to a *nagomi* relationship with them. Indeed, *nagomi*, the Japanese concept of harmony and co-existence, is a great principle to be applied in the alignment of your emotions. In the way of *nagomi*, you do not deny, suppress or try to annihilate something that is potentially negative. Rather, you acknowledge its existence and accept the fact that you have emotions such as anger and jealousy alongside more positive ones. By aligning your emotions with broader values and considerations you make your life robust and affirmative.

As I explored in the previous chapter, we cannot always distinguish between what we can control and what we cannot; there will always be some uncertainty. And where there is uncertainty, emotion naturally gets involved. In fact, certain emotions are reactions to uncertainties in life. We get angry when, for example, someone says something nasty about us unexpectedly. When that remark is predictable, we might still feel bad but we do not get that angry. Anxiety, too, is a typical reaction to uncertainty – you might feel it, for example, when you're watching a horror movie and ominous music suggests the imminent appearance of a monster. Fear is also a quite natural reaction towards the unknown, especially in a situation where you might be facing possible death, the ultimate uncertainty.

So, one stoic trick to reduce negative emotions and uncertainty, is to start from the assumption that your life is going to be difficult – really quite arduous – and that you will have to endure and muddle through. This stoic assumption, if it turns out to be the case, will help you to cope with what comes your way, because you will be well prepared. If, on the other hand, things turn out not to be as hard as you imagined, you can bask in the unexpected sunshine. The worst thing would be to anticipate things to be easy and, when taken by surprise by unexpected difficulties, to react with an uncontrollable surge of negative emotions such as anxiety and anger.

This Stoic ethos of starting from the assumption of difficulty is very much woven into the fabric of Japanese culture. Perhaps because of the frequent occurrence of such natural disasters as earthquakes, tsunamis and typhoons, the Japanese have assumed the attitudes of *gaman* (endurance) and *ganbaru* (making efforts) as default. If your expectations are low, then you can enjoy the sunshine more. The explosive joy the Japanese people exhibit at *hanami* (admiring the cherry blossoms) every spring can be explained, in part, by such a stoic assumption.

The Korakuen garden in Tokyo, built by Tokugawa

Yorifusa, the eleventh son of the great samurai warrior and shogun Tokugawa Ieyasu, is a place of serene and simple beauty. 'Koraku' literally means 'pleasure later', and symbolizes the philosophy of Tokugawa Ieyasu, whose rule opened a period of peace and stability for Japan (1603–1868). A shogun in Ieyasu's time could enjoy all life's pleasures, if he so wished, yet Ieyasu famously likened life to 'a long-distance journey carrying a heavy weight'.

Maybe Ieyasu's attitude towards life was conditioned by the sheer lack of predictability in the existence of a samurai warrior, where today's friend might be tomorrow's enemy. Stoic writers, from Seneca, Epictetus and Marcus Aurelius to their modern colleague Nelson Mandela, have all touched on the issue of unpredictability. Surely one of the hardest things you would psychologically face in prison would be the uncertainty of your fate. Mandela did not know how long he would be imprisoned. One coping mechanism he used was to treat it as an opportunity for learning. Mandela said, 'It is in the character of growth that we should learn from both pleasant and unpleasant experiences. Indeed, if you can face imprisonment with the spirit of learning and personal growth, you can overcome the extreme uncertainties involved.' Stoicism is an attitude. By facing the uncertainties, no matter what, you can learn and personally grow.

Socrates, the father of Stoic thinking, also showed us how to deal with the predictable and unpredictable in life. Indeed, the very idea of the Socratic method is founded on the assumption of open conversation, without any fixed goal or set of correct answers, which inevitably leads to unpredictable conclusions. If we stick to a certain set of ideas, we might get stability, but not learning or spiritual growth. It is no wonder Socrates' Stoic attitude was unsettling for some people in society. Even today, we see people who question the status quo becoming involved in controversies and being attacked. An open attitude can open a Pandora's box of uncertainty, but one we actually require for our spiritual growth.

In order to understand how we may face emotion in appropriate ways, we need to look at the brain's reaction to the uncertainties we encounter in life. Neuroscientists sometimes liken the brain to a time machine. Our memories preserve something of our experiences and effectively take us back to the past. As, from an evolutionary point of view, we are adapted to be able to look to the future (for obvious reasons: to ward off possible threats), the brain, our time machine, effectively tries to travel to the future by running an internal model which predicts what is going to happen by tapping into its storage of memories from the past. Taking advantage of regularities in past events, it makes an educated guess. The neural circuits for predicting the future and those for remembering the past are placed near each other in the brain's network, and they function closely together. This is why we sometimes experience the uncanny feeling that we have lived the present moment and its immediate future before. As the brain tries to retrieve relevant information about what will happen in the current situation, prediction and recollection can be mixed up, giving one the occasional but vivid experience of *déjà vu*.

Of course, it is, in general, impossible to predict the future, due partly to the fact that the world is subject to the dynamical chaos that I mentioned in Chapter 1 (see p. 5). And yet, even with this knowledge, our brains still try to raise the accuracy of prediction by making a statistical inference based on past events.

In this way, the brain is working a little like a generative AI system. OpenAI's ChatGPT which went viral in 2023, is an instance of a predictive machine based on statistical learning. By studying a very large database of what humans have written, ChatGPT can make predictions for the next chunk of words based on an initial input (called prompts). This AI model is known as next token prediction (on account of the fact that words and phrases are represented as tokens).

Needless to say, our brain function is capable of much more than a generative AI system. Indeed, while the outputs of ChatGPT and other Large Language Models (LLMs) or generative AIs in general are impressive, they lack something of the individual uniqueness of real human language. The outputs of LLMs are, in a sense, statistical golden means based on a large chunk of data, and so provide a reasonable representation of what humans would typically say or write in natural language. The individual output of human language, however, is marked by a fundamental unpredictability. There is a butterfly in the neural circuits of humans. When we speak, sometimes the butterfly flaps its wings in unexpected ways, surprising not only the listener but also the speaker.

Unconscious processes also play a part, so that in cases of the famous 'Freudian slip', people say socially upsetting things, which happen to reveal some deep truths of the unconscious.

Jeffrey Hinton, widely regarded as the Godfather of AI for his pioneering research into deep learning, once likened AIs to a butterfly. In March 2023, he tweeted: 'Caterpillars extract nutrients which are then converted into butterflies. People have extracted billions of nuggets of understanding and GPT-4 is humanity's butterfly.' A tweet in response likened Hinton to the Bob Dylan of AI. Maybe he is.*

Hinton's poetic language might leave a lasting impression, but it is debatable whether generative AIs as they stand have the same capacity. There might not be sufficient interesting unpredictability in their outputs. This is probably why people sometimes feel output from generative AIs tends to be bland, lacking that spark of individuality. As we try to design AIs that are capable of creativity, this absence of interesting unpredictability, or butterflies, could become an essential issue.

---

* In 2024, Hinton received the Nobel Prize in Physics, not in Literature, for his pioneering work in deep learning.

As the Lebanese-American mathematician and essayist Nassim Nicholas Taleb described in his book *The Black Swan*, there are certain world events which even experts are unable to predict. The Black Monday stock-market crash in 1987 was one of them. The 9/11 attacks on the World Trade Center in 2001 were another. The Covid-19 outbreak, from the beginning of 2020, is the latest unnerving example. The term 'black swan' comes from the unexpected discovery of black-coloured swans in Australia in 1697, and it has come to symbolize events that occur unexpectedly and out of the blue. The Europeans were so impressed to find that not all swans were white they named the place of discovery the Swan River.

While the brain tries to predict the future by delving into the past – making its own next token prediction – it needs to deal with the uncertain nature of the real world around us. Luckily, we have brain circuits tuned to deal with unexpected things. The emotional circuits centred around the amygdala react to surprising events fast, conditioning the neocortex – which usually conducts detailed analysis more slowly – to treat surprising information in a swift and effective manner. In addition, the amygdala sends a signal to the nearby hippocampus, the centre for memory, so that processing the incoming information can be given priority. Emotionally salient events are thus processed with special weight in the brain. This accounts for the fact that people vividly remember where they were when they first heard about the 9/11 attacks, for example, but do not tend to recall with equal clarity what happened to them one day earlier on 10 September 2001.

It's reassuring to know that by the nature of the human brain, we are mentally set up to handle the unexpected. In the prefrontal cortex, the brain's centre for handling attention, working memory, judgment and choice, there are networks of circuits specially tuned to novel stimuli. The anterior cingulate cortex (ACC), the brain's alarm centre, is activated when something unexpected happens. The signal is then relayed to the dorsolateral prefrontal cortex (DLPFC), which is the brain's executive centre. The ACC sets out the alarm that something requiring attention is happening: the DLPFC then recruits the brain's various circuits to process and analyze the incoming information, making appropriate judgments, and taking action if necessary.

As we go about our lives, we cannot simply avoid uncertainty. Instead, paradoxically, we need to seek it out in order to thrive. Indeed, a hallmark of humanity is that we are a species endowed with an adventurous spirit. Rather than freezing ourselves into non-action in the face of the unknown, we need to explore the large and small, near and far, searching for unknown continents, interacting with strangers, going to the moon and even dreaming of becoming a Martian someday. According to some Hollywood films, it is already happening.

Emotions are natural reactions to uncertainties so we need to welcome them or at least embrace them. Emotions help us to face life's uncertainties in creative and proactive ways, so that we may trailblaze in untrodden territories, proceed in the blue ocean of opportunities. The fact that we humans have a multitude of emotions – for example, hope, courage, joy, expectation, anxiety, fear, sadness, disappointment, etc. – means that we have so many different ways to configure the brain's circuits of cognition and action. Indeed, contrary to the popular misconception that a Stoic is devoid of emotions, it is quite stoic to experience a rich repertoire of emotions in dealing with life's varying situations, some of which are arduous and difficult. Emotions are a Stoic's coping mechanism and strategy.

It is important to realize here that human emotions are ultimately private and thus define a person's unique individuality in an era where people tend to be treated as data. In this digital age, the default assumption is that information can be shared and analyzed within the network, but emotions, by their very nature, cannot be always shared. In that sense, emotions are different from typical information. For example, loneliness is something that, by definition, cannot be shared, precisely because you're on your own. In particular, the loneliness you might feel when you sense that your life is finally ending cannot be shared, and yet this is a destiny that will come to us all someday.

A Japanese *waka* poem by the famous medieval poet Ariwara no Narihira, the swan song placed at the very end of his magnum opus *The Tales of Ise*, which contains about 200 brilliantly crafted *waka* poems, beautifully summarizes this feeling:

I knew I'd have to walk on the path
we all must finally take,
but I had no idea
it would be tomorrow,
much less today.

A few hundred years later, the haiku master Matsuo Basho's last haiku read:

Sick on a journey,
my dreams wander
the withered fields.

Emotions can trigger these poignant observations about life, without which one's brief existence on earth would be so much poorer. It is only with the help of emotions that we can appreciate and taste life in the full. For a Stoic, therefore, there is no reason why emotions should be suppressed and avoided. To be in constant turmoil in the great ocean of emotion is a difficult way to be, but for us humans there is no other option.

CHAPTER 4

The challenge of interpretation

When you read Marcus Aurelius' *Meditations*, you get the feeling that he was always trying to interpret his own life in positive, robust and proactive ways. As a Roman emperor, he must have experienced various dramas, some of them quite unnerving and distressing. During his reign (AD 161–180), Marcus Aurelius fought the Roman–Parthian War and Marcomannic Wars, while the Germanic peoples started to exert their influence on the borders of the Roman Empire. As the Roman emperor in the latter days of *Pax Romana*, Marcus Aurelius must have observed many troubling symptoms of the ailing Empire, but he carried on, while presumably occasionally affected by his own personal affairs, not to mention the outbreak of the Antonine Plague, which claimed the life of Lucius Verus, who co-reigned with him as Roman emperor.

One of the inspirations a modern reader can take from *Meditations* is that of positive interpretation. Indeed, the ability to interpret an objective fact is a creative and affirmative action that can greatly enrich the life cf a Stoic. Given a certain situation, there is always more than one way to interpret a fact. For example, one could say that the glass is half empty or that there is still half the water left. You could be lamenting that you have grown old or say that today you are the youngest in the remaining days of your life, no matter how old you actually are and how aged you might personally feel or, perhaps more importantly for many people, how old the people around you think you are. When you make a mistake, you may lament it as a failure or welcome it as a valuable learning opportunity. Scoring ten out of ten is great, but it might also mean there's no room for further improvement. So next time you score low, say, three out of ten, you could smile and say that there is scope for huge growth. When people around you do not appreciate you, it is natural to be disappointed; alternatively, you could take it as a sign that you're quite unique . . .

In fact, being a one and only is a huge plus in this age, when AIs can process the statistics of a huge database of human behaviour and provide the optimum golden mean as easily as water flowing from the tap. Being a model student at school used to be the key to a successful career; nowadays, a model student runs the risk of becoming a commodity, competing in a losing battle with AI. Today, being a maverick, an outlier far from the masses, could be potentially more rewarding, although it might take some wisdom to muddle through (with a little help from Stoicism). In this situation, the Stoic way of interpreting your life can be a game-changer, turning a mediocre personal trait into a star quality. Indeed, in the coming years, we may need Stoicism to turn every stone of personal uniqueness into gold.

The ability to reinterpret or reappraise the status quo certainly helps you to go about life with a positive and pro-active perspective. When something happens, depending on your interpretation, it may become a comedy or a tragedy or both. That was perhaps the problem facing Romeo and

Juliet. If the young lovers' parents had had the wisdom to look at their children's decisions from a Stoic point of view, and interpreted their situation in positive light – for example, by seeing the romance as an opportunity to bridge the divide between their families – the couple could have been happily living together when Romeo was at the Beatlesque age of sixty-four. Perhaps they should have read *Meditations*.

Interpreting adversarial circumstances in a positive light can engender robustness and creativity in life. Japanese anime has now come to international prominence, but its origin was not at all initiated on a tailwind. Compared to their competitors at Disney, the animators working in the pioneering days of Japanese anime had neither monetary nor human resources. In particular, they had to work with fewer frames per second due to their limited budget. But their ingenuity in the face of this constraint led to the genre's uniquely artistic expressions (and worldwide recognition of the Japanese word *anime* as a label, derived from shortening the English word animation). And it all originated from a Stoic spirit.

Nintendo, the Japanese company universally known for video games featuring characters such as Super Mario Bros, started out manufacturing and producing Japanese traditional playing cards, *hanafuda* (literally, flower cards), and went on to produce Western-style playing cards featuring Disney characters. When faced with little scope for growth in this particular market, Hiroshi Yamauchi, the third president of Nintendo, made the decision to transform the company into a video-game franchise, and the rest is history. To make a dramatic turnaround within the constraints surrounding a corporation was an expression of a truly Stoic spirit. Even the company name, Nintendo, which means leaving luck to heaven, is in alignment with the Stoic philosophy.

As you will gather, how one responds to life's events is a central theme of Stoicism. In the modern world, as we have discussed, outcomes are never certain. Indeed, uncertainty is the only certainty that we face every day. In the age we live in, artificial intelligence is increasingly making situations surrounding our lives, jobs and social structure intractable, while the globalization of economy and culture means everything is increasingly connected, so that we cannot fall back on the comfort of our local environments. Interpreting what happens to us has become a busy and muti-faceted job for each one of us.

But luckily, as with our response to surprise, our brains are, again, configured to help us survive. Cognitive reappraisal is a wonderful function of the brain, involving the prefrontal cortex and other brain areas to reinterpret what is happening to us. By processing a different narrative version of a life event in the prefrontal cortex, we may reduce negative emotions and lower activity in the emotion centre, the amygdala. How might you do this specifically? As an example, when someone says negative things about you, instead of taking it person-ally, you could consider the circumstances that induced the speaker's attitude – say, his or her own feelings of insecurity. In a heated argument, instead of focusing on the negative emotions being triggered, you could, perhaps, consider the benefits of exchanging ideas that would eventually facilitate arriving at a reasonable conclusion. Cognitive reappraisal, thus executed by the brain's prefrontal cortex, helps you to streamline your emotions by bringing your affective reactions into alignment with your best practice as a human being.

The challenge of interpretation applies not only to external events, but also to one's own emotions, and here, too, Marcus Aurelius shows the way. As you turn the pages of *Meditations*, it becomes clear that that the Stoic emperor was not an emotionless person, nor someone who suppressed emotions. Rather, he knew how to interpret them. Indeed, Marcus Aurelius was a master of interpreting emotions caused by life's adversarial events. If, as I argued in the previous chapter, emotions are natural reactions to uncertainties in life that we need to welcome and accommodate, Stoicism is a process of dynamically interpreting incidents, one's emotions and even the sensory pleasures that come one's way.

There are so many instances in life when interpretation can turn a negative emotion into a proactive perspective. For example, you might feel jealous when someone becomes successful. You might even be carried away by your jealousy. You might start criticizing them or declare that their success is without value. This is the famous 'sour-grapes' grudge from 'The Fox and the Grapes' fable in *Aesop's Fables*. When you are in the grip of this grudge, you cannot see things clearly. You will not be able to make fair judgments about yourself and other people, and life typically goes downhill.

When you see the toxic effects of jealousy, your instinct might be to suppress it or to stay away from comparison altogether. But if you know how to apply cognitive reappraisal, you do not necessarily have to suppress the emotion. Instead, when you feel jealousy, you could interpret it as a chance to perceive something that you'd secretly hoped to achieve yourself. Your version may not be the exact copy of what the person you are jealous of has achieved; it may just be something of a similar nature, in terms of social consequences or the kinds of ability required. But once you realize that there is an element there that you would like to achieve for yourself, you will be able to start making straightforward and honest efforts towards reaching that goal, instead of being burnt by your jealousy, calling the grapes sour and rubbishing the successful person.

In addition, if the successful person in question is someone close to you, you could make the following assessment. Sure, if you experience the glamour of success close by, you may feel the pain of feeling inferior in comparison. But on the other hand, a success within the proximity of your social network could mean more opportunity for you. The successful person might introduce to you some important people. You might learn the mindset, patterns of conduct and ways of life that correlate with success from close up. You are more likely to be invited to a luxurious meal, attend a party with influential people, receive precious gifts and get in touch with a valuable source of information. Thus, you have nothing to lose and everything to gain when someone close to you becomes successful. If you were only able to overcome your jealousy, which, to be honest, is a kind of panic reaction, you would be pleased rather than upset.

It is worth noting that the reappraisal of emotions that I am discussing here is a way of keeping your personal integrity. When you're jealous, you become somewhat upset, and you momentarily become a person you really are not. From the Stoic perspective, it is the disruption of personal integrity that is the problem with many emotions such as fear, anxiety, anger and malice. The great job of the human brain's prefrontal cortex is to help you find your way back to your own self, not by suppressing negative emotions but by streamlining your cognitive judgments – making sense of what has happened and is happening to you, and eventually aligning yourself with the better person that you originally were. Indeed, it could be said that the brain's prefrontal cortex is where Stoicism resides.

It is not only negative emotions that can throw us off course. There is plenty of anecdotal evidence that when people experience positive emotions such as pleasure, joy, curiosity, satisfaction, a sense of wonder and even awe, shit can happen. People often quarrel, crash into each other, have arguments, disagree and even break up at the pinnacle of achievements, or in moments of happiness and joy. For example, boasting about one's achievements could alienate even those close to us. This rather counterintuitive phenomenon makes sense when you realize that people equally tend to lose their personal integrity when they experience extremely positive emotions. They forget themselves, neglect paying due respect to others and can go through a flash of selfishness. Losing one's personal integrity can turn a celebratory situation into a dire nightmare. Stoicism is about keeping your personal integrity and seeing clearly the shape of your soul.

The Japanese traditional philosophy of life, *ikigai*, is of great help when it comes to keeping your personal integrity intact. *Ikigai* literally means 'reason for living'. In the context of Stoicism, *ikigai* provides the feeling that what you are doing aligns with your perception of yourself and how you want to relate to others and to society at large. In the brain, the insula – the area implicated in processing related to emotions, bodily sensations, self-awareness, interpersonal relationships and reward – is likely to be one of the centres for *ikigai*.

One great thing about *ikigai* is that it is not one of those proxy goals which typically exert a great influence on the modern man. (Here, a proxy goal is not something that is inherent and central to your life, but something you might have set as a tentative and practical purpose, a goal laid on you by the expectations of society. For example, many people equate success with money. While practically speaking, money is great, it is not life's ultimate or most essential goal. It is quite conceivable that you may have a lot of money and yet feel miserably unhappy. The same goes for success. If you succeed in your work, that is quite wonderful. However, success might bring about turmoil and mis-alignment and could even erode your precious inner self. Many people strive to attain social status but discover on arrival there is no pot of gold at the rainbow's end.) In life, there are many proxy goals, such as money, success, status and fame, but attaining these does not necessarily mean you will be happy. More importantly, trying to achieve proxy goals can disrupt your personal integrity and change the shape of your soul. If you read *Meditations*, it is clear that Marcus Aurelius is acutely aware of the futility of proxy goals and the dangers of disrupting of personal integrity, although he might not use those exact words.

Ikigai is helpful because it is self-referential – your own 'reason for living'. It is not a goal you pursue as a means of enriching your life; *ikigai is* your life. From that perspective, it could be anything small, like having a coffee in the morning, or something big, like a great achievement you would like to accomplish in your career. I, myself, have both small and large *ikigai*. My small *ikigai* concerns itself with a little creature. I am based in Tokyo, Japan and when I go for a morning run, my heart starts dancing and I feel great joy when I see a butterfly flying around in the park. This butterfly moment (as opposed to the 'butterfly effect' of chaos theory!) is relevant for me personally as I used to study butterflies as a kid. Now, I know many people don't care about butterflies. Many cannot even distinguish a butterfly from a moth (can you?), but that is quite all right because each person can have *ikigai* in their own unique way.

My big *ikigai* is to understand how consciousness arises from brain activities. When I was thirty-one, riding on a train in Tokyo, I realized that my conscious experience is composed of sensory qualities, or qualia. Ever since, trying to understand the enigma of consciousness has been my biggest *ikigai*, although without success so far.

Having a spectrum of *ikigai*, from the small to the large, private to public, or from butterflies to qualia in my case, helps us to hold on to our integrity. And in the world we live in, positively interpreting events, reappraising our emotions and maintaining our personal integrity will become ever more important as we go through a time of great social change.

CHAPTER 5

Accepting one's uniqueness

One of the key tenets of Stoicism is to accept oneself. Accepting oneself does not necessarily mean resignation, submission, fatalism or giving up hope of improving one's life. Indeed, to acknowledge and then go along with one's own peculiarities is an active process, in which one can be proactive and creative. Importantly, one might even change for the better in that process. It is far from stagnating in the status quo.

Marcus Aurelius writes repeatedly about self-understanding and self-acceptance in *Meditations*. Socrates, the father of the Stoic tradition, in his Socratic dialogues, also stresses the importance of the philosophical maxim 'know thyself', which was originally an inscription in the Temple of Apollo in ancient Greece. It could be said that Socrates was devoted to knowing himself till the last day of his life.

In today's cultural climate, in which it is politically correct to stress the importance of DEI (diversity, equity and inclusion), accepting one's own unique conditions sounds almost like a cliche, hardly worthy of careful study. However, the difference in our individual situations is actually one of the most overlooked truths in life. We often fail to realize just how different people are in their configuration of mind and body. There are literally millions of possible conditions in millions of people, and each person is uniquely optimized and challenged to pursue various goals. In order to understand this point, you need look no further than the popular entertainment and pastime of our time, sports.

Sport is a perfect platform from which to see Stoicism in action. Indeed, many professional sportspeople, from footballers to baseballers, runners to swimmers, are known for their Stoic philosophy and behaviour; in fact, the popular perception is that you need to have the stoic ability to push through discomfort to achieve a high level of excellence. I would agree, but from a different stoic perspective: to excel, you need efficiently to employ your mind and body in ways that align with what you've been given. The Stoicism here is in the alignment of the optimum performance required and the unique conditions of one's mind and body

Let's look at the Olympics. The Olympics were first held in ancient Greece from 776 BC to AD 393, encompassing a period of more than 1,100 years. During that time athletes competed in many categories of sport, including running, combat, discus throwing, javelin throwing, long jump, horse and chariot racing. The familiar images of athletes competing in these games, as represented by ancient Greek statues and paintings, conjure up the idea of a perfect body. Indeed, in the modern Olympics (the games were revived in 1896, the Paris Olympics in 2024 being the twenty-eighth games since the revival), the pentathlon competition still maintains this ideal of an athletic body that excels in all competitions. It has perhaps become our default assumption, as if there is a sports version of a Renaissance man. In fact, nothing could be further from the truth.

One of the unique aspects of the Olympics is the

convention of all the participating athletes living in a single Olympic village. In other international competitions, the athletes just arrive at the site, staying at their own hotels. Quite a few of them are rich, supported by lucrative sponsorships, and stay in luxury hotel suites, with dedicated staff accompanying them at every step. In contrast, the hospitality at the Olympic village is quite humble and subdued, although certainly more than adequate. Everyone shares the same kind of room, bed and catering experiences. Even if you are a top-tournament tennis pro or a major league baseball player, you are treated on equal footing with those athletes from less high-profile competitions. At the Olympic village, every athlete is in the same boat, thanks to the Stoic ideology of the idealistic and laudable Olympic movement.

That an Olympic village should have a Stoic outlook is fitting, considering the fact that the Olympic games share the same ancient Greek origin as the Stoic school of thought founded by Zeno of Citium. Given the timeline of the ancient Olympics and Socrates' life (470–399 BC) it is quite possible that the Greek philosopher was familiar with the festival of sport held every four years. Although we do not know whether Marcus Aurelius ever competed in the ancient Olympics, he showed an interest and trained in sports such as boxing and wrestling, and we do know that Nero, another Roman emperor, was awarded medals in the games. It is thus fitting to associate ancient Olympics with Stoicism.

But the Stoic nature of the Olympic village runs deeper still, according to a friend of mine, the Japanese hurdler Dai Tamesue, who has competed in the Olympics and has twice won a bronze medal in the World Athletics. By far the most striking thing about seeing everyone gathered at the Olympic village, Tamesue says, is the fact that it becomes obvious that there are all kinds of people competing as athletes, with all kinds of bodily configurations. The Greek statues of the earliest Olympians might suggest that a perfect body is required for every competition, but that is very far from the reality. Instead, the optimum physical features for an athlete appear to be strikingly different depending on the nature of the competition. In fact, it is debatable whether there was ever a single converging form of 'ideal' human body in the first place. A short-distance runner looks different from a long-distance one. An excellent javelin thrower will be configured differently from, say, a basketball player or a swimmer. A weightlifter might share some physical features with a judo champion, but there would be subtle and important differences, which, crucially, would count when competing at the highest level. It is wonderful, Tamesue says, that at the Olympic village you see a true celebration of the diversity of human forms.

Tamesue himself has a both painful and glorious personal story which illustrates the different physical gears required for different competitions and the Stoicism of embracing one's unique personal conditions. When he was younger, Tamesue used to compete in the 100 metres. In his early teens, his record was improving to the extent that, at certain periods, he was faster than Usain Bolt at the same age. However, as he grew up, his times started to get sluggish, and despite incredible efforts on his part, he could not improve them. That was when he decided to change to the 400-metre hurdle in order to stand a realistic chance of winning in an international competition.

According to Tamesue, there appear to be specific bodily configurations that help you become a 100-metre champion.

While there is, as yet, no scientifically established under-standing of what these parameters are, top athletes like Tamesue intuitively seem to know them from their own experience. 'It is about the shape of the heels, the flexibility of the joints and the length of the thighs,' he told me. 'Your body needs to be configured in just the right way to be a 100-metre run champion.'

Tamesue's observation shines a light on the relationship between what we are born with and what we acquire through effort. It is wonderful to say that we can be anyone we want to be and make great efforts accordingly, but at the same time we need to be realistic. This is the spirit of Stoicism reflected in Marcus Aurelius's writing. If you are a Stoic, you should be audacious about pursuing your possibilities, but also mindful of possible limitations.

It is crucial to say here that you cannot know your limi-tations unless you try hard – *very* hard, in fact. Tamesue learned his limitations the hard way, only *after* trying his utmost to excel in the 100-metre dash. Although he is aware of the possible limits of his own physical configuration, the current status of sports science is such that nobody can be sure if their genetic and physical make-up are up for a specific challenge unless they try, sometimes to the very highest level. There is, as yet, no test that will tell us whether a sportsperson is fitted for a particular task. Only experience will show.

Challenges due to one's unique limitations can occur in mental activities as well as physical exercises. Each of us experiences our own particular difficulties. Some of us are good at one thing and others excel in another. Life is about trying to discover our own configuration, through trial and error. And even then, we may not know if we are a good fit or not, sometimes right up until the last day of our lives.

There is something intriguing about the unique package of merits and shortcomings of an individual. Even Albert Einstein famously expressed doubts about his ability in mathematics. He once confessed that he did not intuitively know which field of mathematics he should pursue. He likened himself to the famous fable of Buridan's ass, in which an ass (donkey), placed between two equally desirable items, such as hay and water, cannot decide which way to go, and eventually dies of hunger and thirst.

Needless to say, compared to the typical person on the

street, Einstein did have exceptional abilities to handle mathematics. How else could he have developed the general theory of relativity, which required a mastery of tensor calculus and non-Euclidian geometry? What Einstein probably wanted to say was that, compared to his genius for applying relevant intuitions to physics, which led to world-transforming discoveries, his capabilities in pure mathematics were limited. Like Tamesue, who pivoted from the 100-metre dash to the 400-metre hurdle, Einstein stayed away from trying to excel in pure mathematics and concentrated his efforts on physics, discovering the famous equation $E = mc^2$, transfiguring the way we look at the world we live in beyond recognition.

Each one of us is empowered in some ways and limited in others. What makes us unique is not our talents (we might share these with others) but the configuration of talents and shortcomings within us. In order to succeed in this world, we need to see ourselves clearly. It is quite a stoic thing to do – to acknowledge one's limitations and yet try one's very best within them. It does not do to pursue the mirage of the perfect Greek body or its mental equivalent. Stoicism is about aligning yourself with your own unique conditions and selecting what you do accordingly.

In our modern world, the image of a Stoic is often associated with austerity, and perhaps even a hint of monoculture. When you hear the word 'stoic', you do not typically think of a colourful multitude of unique characters; rather, it seems to suggest a world made of black, white and some grey (and not even fifty shades of grey). But if to be Stoic is to accept one's own peculiarities, then, the particular manner in which one exerts oneself might be quite different from person to person. In this sense, each of us is a Stoic in our own way and being so is a celebration of the diversity of life. There are so many different ways one can be aligned that Stoicism is very far from the monocultural image of austerity prevalent today.

I once had the rare and joyous privilege of interviewing Kim Peek, who was the inspiration for the autistic-savant character in the film *Rain Man*, played by Dustin Hoffman. He was accompanied by his father, Fran Peek. Kim was known for his incredible ability to memorize things. Indeed, once Kim learned something, he never forgot it. When Kim was young, Fran came to notice that some of the books in his house were turned upside down. Puzzled, he did some investigating and learned that these were books Kim had finished scanning. From birth, Kim's brain lacked a *corpus callosum*, a structure connecting the right and left hemispheres of the brain. As a consequence, Kim was able to scan the left and right pages of a book at the same time. Once scanned, Kim remembered every detail of what he had read, verbatim, without any errors – the striking capability depicted in *Rain Man*.

It was fascinating to witness Kim's memory capacity at work. If you asked him a question, it led to a chain reaction of associated memories, and Kim would keep bubbling away, mentioning things at an incredible speed. For example, if you asked a question about a former Yankees player, Kim would answer with a factoid about him, then he would say something about New York, mentioning the nickname 'Big Apple', and go on to say that the apple cultivar Granny Smith originated in Australia, going from there to koalas. While it was evident that there was no controlling his responses, Kim's chain reaction of memory went full speed in unimaginable and unpredictable directions. Kim's physical behaviour was also non-typical – he was constantly moving around, never standing still.

Fran Peek carried around their Oscar statuette whenever he went somewhere in town with Kim. Then if, for example, Kim behaved in a non-typical way in a restaurant, and drew the attention of nearby customers, Fran would show them the Oscar, and explain proudly that the film *Rain Man*, based on his son, Kim, had won the Academy Award for Best Original Screenplay. Then people understood instantly. The statuette was given to the co-writers of the film, Ronald Bass and Barry Morrow, who kindly passed it on to Fran. Fran said their Oscar was likely to have been held by more people in the world than any other.

Kim's story demonstrates another element of Stoicism. It is evident that it was Fran's love and dedication that helped Kim's unique individuality to flourish. In order to celebrate the diversity of life, we sometimes need to collaborate and help each other. Stoicism is definitely not always a solitary affair but can be about helping others to align with their own uniqueness, too.

Stoicism's respect for each of our unique qualities is a

celebration of life's diversity in general. If we broaden our perspective to non-human species, each biological species is Stoic in its own way, from earthworms to exotic birds, and from microorganisms to a giant blue whale. Stoicism could be about the diverse ways in which life forms on Earth have evolved and are evolving. The Earth's ecological system can hold so many different species because each knows its niche in the environment and does not overstep it. In order to co-exist harmoniously within the ecological system, we need to make intelligent use of our individual resources, such as physiology, energy and motion. In this sense, acceptance of one's own conditions and embracing our unique contribution to the world is a form of alignment and a manifestation of the Stoic way of life.

There is no perfect physique fit for all sports, and the same goes for intelligence, personality or character. In life, there is no one-size-fits-all. To be Stoic is to align with one's own condition, and let others do the same. In doing so, we are celebrating the diversity of life. In the final passage of his magnum opus *On the Origin of Species*, Charles Darwin wrote movingly about the world's 'endless forms, most beautiful and most wonderful'. This could well have been a statement about Stoicism. This world contains endless forms of being stoic, most beautiful and most wonderful. Indeed, *On the Origin of Species* could be considered as an essential work in the long lines of works that have carried the torch of Stoicism since the ancient days of Socrates.

CHAPTER 6

Celebrating life's diversity while accepting its limits

I once had the honour of hosting the physicist Sir Roger Penrose (who went on to win the Nobel Prize in Physics, 2020, 'for the discovery that black hole formation is a robust prediction of the general theory of relativity') for an evening in Japan's ancient capital, Kyoto. I knew Penrose from my days as a postdoc at the University of Cambridge and he had come to give a lecture at the Kyoto International Conference Centre. I took him for a *kaiseki* dinner. Japanese *kaiseki* cooking is famous for its ravishing use of ingredients taken from nature. In a typical meal, over several courses, the customer will be treated to up to, say, thirty different delicacies, ranging from fresh fish to a perfectly ripe piece of fruit – a celebration of the diversity you find in nature. On that evening, we discussed various things from geometry, gravitation, consciousness and, needless to say, the sheer culinary delight of *kaiseki*. It was so fascinating and rewarding to witness my companion's eyes light up in the face of the miscellaneous ingredients put before him. On that evening, at least, it was *kaiseki* that was a black hole of attention for Sir Roger Penrose.

Many chefs in the world today regard *kaiseki* as one of the most refined forms of cooking. It might, therefore, seem too luxurious for the humble spirit of Stoicism, but nothing could be further from the truth. In actuality, *kaiseki* is the apotheosis of Stoicism, as every ingredient is received from nature with gratitude. There is no hubris on the part of the chef, who applies a minimum of seasonings and sauces to cook and prepare the freshest ingredients, even though it takes ingenuity and effort to get hold of certain materials, some of which might be highly prized. Using rare or expensive ingredients is not the point, however, although some frivolous customers do make a fuss about it. Indeed, ingredients in their prime season, when they taste the best, will typically be moderately priced, compared to the *hashiri* (start of the season) or *nagori* (end of the season), as I describe in more detail in my book *The Way of Nagomi*. The attitude of the chef in *kaiseki* is always one of gratitude, humility and, if I may add, a sense of wonder.

The most important part of the *kaiseki* approach is that it accepts the limits of the changing seasons. You may take ingredients from nature, and search for them far and wide, but you must not step outside the limits set by nature within the tides of the seasons. The *kaiseki* chef might be extravagant in their exploration of the senses, but only in accordance with what nature has to offer at that moment. In this way, *kaiseki* demonstrates how we can be Stoics, but joyous at the same time, appreciating the sensory pleasures that come our way in this theatre that is life.

The sensory pleasures of *kaiseki* are also a wonderful metaphor for the version of Stoicism humanity could adopt in the coming years. We need not be extravagant, but we can surely be here to enjoy, appreciate and celebrate the diversity of life through our five senses. We could be immersed in the spectrum of sensory pleasures and be satisfied within the limitations of the here and now. When we accept the limits of our own existence, life becomes a celebration of sensory qualia – a striking characteristic of our conscious experience. Here, qualia might be qualities such as the redness of red, the coolness of water and the fragrance of a rose. Qualia cannot be fully described in terms of numbers and equations, the traditional methods employed in science. Understanding how consciousness full of qualia arises from neural activities in the brain is considered to be one of the most challenging problems for science (as well as my personal and ultimate *ikigai*).

This celebration of life through the senses makes Stoicism something that sits outside ideologies and politics, and is applicable across the span of human situations and social contexts. Indeed, Stoicism is a robust principle relevant to any kind of country or situation you might find yourself to be living in. Harvard professor Steven Pinker once expressed an optimistic view of the world, stressing the fact that worldwide more people are getting out of poverty, living in a parliamentary democracy and enjoying higher education. Yet, while such progress for humankind is certainly welcome, the gift of Stoicism, as it becomes an essential wisdom of our times, lies in the fact that it can be applied by anyone, living in any culture, under any system of government. Even if the particular condition we find ourselves in might not always optimal, Stoicism shows us a way to proceed.

On a personal level, every one of us is born into a particular familial background; some of us are lucky, some of us are not. Marcus Aurelius was born into a web of connections which eventually meant he became emperor of the Roman Empire. Epictetus was born into a situation where he found himself a slave, although later in life he became a free man. Both of them went on to write texts (in the case of Marcus Aurelius) or have texts written (in the case of Epictetus) that belong to the Stoic canon. Stoicism is an incredibly adaptable attitude towards life, and no matter where you are, in whatever circumstances you find yourself, you can always find a stoic way to muddle through. In this respect, Stoicism is wider than democracy, liberalism and happiness combined. This is quite important, as we find ourselves in a world full of political division. It is not Stoic to subscribe to a particular opinion, no matter how justifiable it may appear to be, while ignoring the existence of members of your community. (You need only remember how Socrates lived in order to realize that you have to embrace and communicate with your neighbours to be a Stoic.) Stoicism is more aligned with life itself than with any ideology that might capture people's hearts (often, with the benefit of hindsight, to little avail in the end).

On a fundamental level, none of us lives outside the limits of the laws of nature, or is unaffected by the great procession of the universe. Indeed, Stoicism is ultimately the question of how to live, given the constraints of this world we find ourselves in. At a time when artificial intelligence is making great progress, we might sometimes be under the illusion that in the coming years our human capacities will be so greatly improved and augmented that there will be no limits to what we can do. But to assume that we can overcome all our limitations is to behave like the legendary King Gilgamesh who, having enjoyed all possible worldly fame and power, went on a journey in search of immortality. Gilgamesh eventually realized that this was beyond his reach; he finally accepted his mortality, and passed away, as every one of us will do someday.

Even placing our unavoidable mortality to one side, we humans are limited in so many other ways. The structure of memory is one of them. Many people would like their memories to have infinite capacity, so that they could perform better in work and live life to the full. Memory is central to our existence as humans – our very notion of life depends on it – and ideally, we would like to remember everything we learn and be able to recall every detail of our lives, so that we could live and relive every moment at will. Yet, we are simply not configured to be capable of such things. And while it is typical for us to lament the poor performance of our memories, especially as we age and mature, even from a vibrant, young age the human memory is limited in both capacity and retention. This is what makes us human – perhaps all too human.

If you examine human memory performance closely, there are so many bottlenecks and loopholes one wonders how we live a civilized life at all. Our memories make us who we are;

nothing is more devastating than the total loss of the capacity for episodic memory, because it damages our sense of who we are as a person. If the hippocampus, the centre for memory in the human brain, is damaged, or there are other dysfunctions in related brain regions, the ability to form new memories can be permanently lost. When that happens, no matter what you go through, it is not going to stay with you. If you go on a trip, for example, irrespective of what you see, hear and eat, regardless of who you meet, what serendipity you encounter, the experiences will pass, just as time passes, and nothing is changed or retrieved. This is an increasingly common experience for many people who suffer from dementia due to conditions such as Alzheimer's.

But the fact is, even with a typically functioning brain, we are destined to forget the majority of what happens to us, no matter how hard we try not to. Various neuroscientific studies suggest that we do not remember the overwhelming majority of what we see. Under experimental conditions, it has been demonstrated that human subjects are not aware when salient features of a visual scene have been changed. For example, if the roof of a house was changed from blue to red, the participants likely wouldn't notice, unless, for some reason or another, their attention was directed to that part of the scene. Intriguingly, when asked whether they thought that they were seeing everything, the subjects tended to answer in the affirmative. The discrepancy between what we believe we experience on one hand and actually remember on the other is one of the greatest enigmas of our lives.

How we live through the stream of consciousness, and how we focus on the here and now are important aspects of Stoicism. Memory is an important element in the Stoic life, because unless we are connected to our past and future through memory, life does not make any sense.

In Marcel Proust's *In Search of Lost Time*, widely regarded as one of the greatest novels of the twentieth century, the protagonist, a young man, looks back on the experiences of his life, many of which have not been happy. He aspires to achieve something in life and searches for social status, fame, wealth and love in his quest for meaning. He is, however, disappointed by all his attempts. Finally, he is saved by an involuntary memory. In a famous scene, he dips a madeleine cake in tea, and that action, and the flavour he experiences in his mouth, lead to a series of recollections of his life so far. The narrator realizes that, despite all his efforts to achieve something, even seemingly trivial experiences can connect him to the rich flow of life.

The Native American psychologist Marigold Linton, a pioneer in the study of autobiographical memory, termed the sudden resurgence of involuntary memories, such as those depicted in Proust's madeleine moment, precious fragments. It is indeed the precious fragments of our mortal lives, as we live through the stream of consciousness, that constitute the celebratory diversity in a Stoic's life.

In Stoicism, when we celebrate the diversity in life, we do so in alignment with the limitations of society, culture and, most importantly, nature, including how our brains are configured to give us memories. Sometimes in that process, self-restraint rather than a carefree spree might be the name of the game. That's why a Stoic might appear to be self-restraining and subdued, even when she or he is actually drinking from life's cup with full joy. A Stoic is aligning with the wider flow of life by focusing on the sensory pleasures of the everyday. Life is finite, and you will not remember everything. However, you can always savour the present, and that is the best you can ever hope to do.

CHAPTER 7

Stoicism and creativity

Nowadays, humans value creativity more than any other trait. Indeed, in recent years, our emphasis on creativity seems to have reached a new dimension. In education, nurturing creativity is regarded as an important priority both for parents wishing to encourage it in their children and in national policy. Certainly, it is prized over rote learning and doing well in test scores. In popular culture, creative people are highly respected, and pop stars, artists, scientists and technologists are revered due to their perceived creativity.

If we were to look for a model of a creative person, perhaps Wolfgang Amadeus Mozart as depicted in the 1984 film *Amadeus* might come to mind. In this classic movie, the eighteenth-century musical prodigy is portrayed as a mischievous and playful character who acts on impulse. In contrast, his competitor Antonio Salieri is depicted as someone with serious intentions, who seldom tells or enjoys jokes, and who is somewhat puzzled and offended by Mozart's exuberant and erratic behaviour. The dynamic of the film centres on the fact that the mischievous Mozart is gifted with divine creativity, while the serious and stubborn Salieri enjoys only a mediocre musical talent.

Some critics have said that this portrayal of the two musicians is neither entirely fair nor historically accurate, especially as regards Salieri. However, the film, and the play on which it was based, became huge hits precisely because Mozart fitted our perception of how a creative genius should be: someone who displays a playful spirit and is disruptive – attributes which are offset and justified by the benefit their talents bring to humanity.

In more recent times, Steve Jobs, whose idiosyncratic behaviour and unpredictable attitude terrified and perhaps alienated some people around him, achieved incredible feats such as the creation of the iPhone format – a style for smartphones that is still prevalent. We like to believe that a creative is someone who challenges the status quo and has no respect for thinking – or behaving – 'inside the box'.

Thus, there is an image problem for Stoics as regards creativity. Put bluntly, a Stoic – seeking balance and practising restraint – does not appear to be creative. Creativity requires a spark of genius, and perhaps an erratic, impulsive nature, which a Stoic surely does not possess. A stoic person can be relied upon for doing routine tasks and setting the record straight, but not for the world-changing works of fascinating innovation that Mozart was capable of producing.

Conclusion: Stoics are not creative.

Stoicism has nothing to do with creativity. Period.

Well, not so fast.

In fact, creative people such as Mozart are very stoic, albeit with different character traits from those we have so far discussed. Indeed, there is a logical reason why a creative genius by necessity has to be Stoic.

Take some famous scientists and inventors, who are often noted for their colourful and eccentric characters. Albert Einstein, for example, did not admire one of his college professors and showed his disrespect, resulting in his failure to get a job at the university. (He discovered the theory of relativity working independently at night, after his day job at the patent office.) The controversial South-African born technologist Elon Musk is famous for his involvement in innovative companies such as PayPal, Tesla, SpaceX, Starlink and OpenAI, alongside more challenging ventures such as Neuralink, HyperLoop, and The Boring Company. Musk has become a household name as an innovator – and as a rule breaker who shows little respect for popular opinion. Yet there is one thing that these very different characters absolutely respect and observe, and that is the laws of physics. Or the laws of nature in general. You can disagree with people's opinions, you can ignore human-made regulations and red tape, but you cannot ignore natural laws. No matter how ingenious you are, you cannot beat the laws of physics.

For example, it is widely accepted that you cannot build a perpetual-motion machine – a machine that can work indefinitely without an external power source – because the laws of thermodynamics forbid it. There have been many claims for successful creations of perpetual-motion machines and many seemingly ingenious approaches but none of them can get round these immutable laws.

Judgments on the feasibility of other inventions might be more ambiguous. For example, within the framework of general theory of relativity, it *might* one day be possible to build a time machine and travel through time. It would create several inconsistencies (one of the most famous being the capacity to travel to the past and kill your father before you are even conceived), but unlike the perpetual-motion machine, the jury is still out on whether it is actually impossible. Other challenges are difficult to judge at this moment in human history. It is not yet clear whether a cure for cancer, dementia or ageing will one day be possible. Many researchers have worked on such audacious projects as superconductivity at room temperature and fusion energy but have not yet succeeded. Perhaps more intriguingly, other inventions look less viable now than was once supposed. It is now not clear whether it will, after all, be possible to build a fully self-driving car, a functioning quantum computer or Artificial General Intelligence (AGI) – three of the most conspicuous challenges that tech enthusiasts such as Elon Musk have been pushing forward in recent years.

But one thing is for sure, when trying to solve these scientific and technological challenges, the character traits of the people involved are not important. The construction of a functioning quantum computer, for example, is known to depend on a process called quantum error correction (QEC), a highly mathematical and technical procedure which would rectify possible errors arising from decoherence. A playful character wouldn't help solve a problem in QEC. At present, there are heated discussions whether Large Language Models (LLMs) would eventually lead to AGI, the Holy Grail of AI research. Here, again, an impulsive researcher waving hands and making jokes would not be much help.

The more you mean business and not just talk, the more you need to delve deeply into the technical details of a system, the more you need Stoicism 100 per cent. Otherwise, what you build will just be a sandcastle blown away by the winds of the world. In this respect, even if their flamboyant speech and behaviour might be frowned upon, a successful inventor/technologist has to be a Stoic, because their approach must be rigorously and stoically logical and observe the laws of physics. And it is not only in the fields of science and technology that this applies. There are similar inner logics and organizations to music. When Mozart composed, there is no doubt he had a stoic understanding and implementation of the inner logic of music, otherwise he could not have been a great composer.

Thus, the popular perception that being Stoic is the antithesis of being creative seems to be misguided. Instead, I would suggest that every creative person is Stoic, or rather should be Stoic, in that she or he must follow an inner logic and organic structure when creating something. Stoicism, in this sense, becomes a necessary condition for being creative. Other personality traits, such as playfulness, disruption and mischief, although they may often accompany a creative person, are entirely optional. It is equally also quite possible, and not infrequent, that an outwardly playful character, lacking inner Stoicism, might be entirely devoid of creativity.

What is crucially important in creativity is inner Stoicism. Everything else is a bonus. In fact, it is conceivable that the characters of Mozart and Salieri in *Amadeus* could have been flipped, so that the serious character composed fantastic music while the mischievous joker entirely lacked any true talent (although as a drama it would not have been as fun).

There is another reason why creative people need to be stoic: the need to overcome difficulties involved. In the field of cognitive science dealing with learning and creativity, there is a concept called 'desirable difficulties', which posits that effective learning processes, and even genius, flourish when we face obstacles – difficulties that eventually, after we have made considerable efforts to overcome them, turn into desirable obstacles with the benefit of hindsight.

In the laboratory, desirable difficulties can be set up and studied by creating reproducible situations involving obstacles to perception. For example, under certain conditions, studying handwritten notes can enhance one's memory compared to a more readable printout. Using hard-to-read fonts might actually result in the learner's performance improving.

Then there are the more psychologically penetrating kinds of difficulty, which nurture the development of unusual talents. Marcus Aurelius certainly had his share of desirable difficulties. The Stoic emperor lived at a difficult time for the Roman Empire, troubled by wars and plague, even if he makes few references to the contemporary affairs of his time in *Meditations*. These troubles may have turned into desirable difficulties, giving rise to his creativity in making and executing policies as the last of the 'Five Good Emperors' and the last emperor of the *Pax Romana*.

One theory on the origin of genius posits that the early death(s) of one or both of parents might contribute to coping abilities that correlate with the development of genius, as premature parental death(s) provide(s) desirable difficulties, albeit tragically. Marcus Aurelius's father died when he was just three years old, and he did not spend much time with his mother, either. The list of geniuses whose parent(s) died prematurely is striking: Aristotle, Robert Boyle, Albert Camus, Nicolaus Copernicus, Marie Curie, Charles Darwin, Robert Hooke, David Hume, Antoine Lavoisier, James Maxwell, Isaac Newton, Friedrich Nietzsche, Blaise Pascal, Linus Pauling, Jean-Jacques Rousseau, Bertrand Russell, Jean-Paul Sartre, Mary Shelley, Adam Smith, Benedict Spinoza, Voltaire – this list is a very small sample – the actual cohort is very big, almost endless.

Life expectancy used to be short, so it is statistically not so surprising that these luminaries suffered the misfortune of premature parental death(s). On the other hand, compared to today, social welfare was almost non-existent, so it is likely that many of these creative geniuses faced tremendous financial and practical difficulties, not to mention the psychological challenges that accompany loss. For example, Isaac Newton had to support himself while studying at the University of Cambridge by doing petty jobs like catering and cleaning at Trinity College. It was only when the University closed because of the Great Plague in 1665–6 that he was forced home to Lincolnshire. Yet that year of isolation turned out to be an *annus mirabilis* (miraculous year) for Newton and humanity. He discovered gravitation, when, legend has it, he saw an apple falling from a tree.

The exact details of the neural mechanisms involved when a talented person overcomes obstacles and turns them into desirable difficulties are not yet known. It is likely that sustainable recruitment of the brain's memory circuits, together with the executive functions involved in choice and action are at play. Memory formation aligned with action happens all the time. In addition, at a time of difficulty and when faced with emotionally disturbing situations, the reappraisal networks of the prefrontal cortex, which support alternative ways to interpret the environment, would be invoked. Thus begins a journey of self-transformation.

In Japanese culture, this attitude of making arduous efforts to muddle through incredible difficulties is called *ganbaru*, literally meaning 'make efforts', as we saw earlier. The importance of *ganbaru* is stressed in many aspects of Japanese society, from the classroom to the workplace, and in business-school texts and manga comic books. As described by Marco Polo (1254–1324), Japan, under the ancient name of Zipangu, used to be considered a land of gold. Perhaps *ganbaru* was how our ancient Japanese forefathers came to strike gold in Japan – literally turning desirable difficulties into golden nuggets.

Bringing about disruptive innovation can create its own difficulties. It can mean running against a strong wind of friction, with people trying to exert Luddite types of opposition. Prometheus, the Greek god who brought fire to humanity, was punished for his ambition by being bound to a rock with an eagle sent to tear out his liver. Even today, the audacious belief that we human beings can overcome the limitations of human existence by technological advancement is sometimes called Promethean. This is the credo of the start-ups in Silicon Valley, exemplified by people like Mark Zuckerberg, Sam Altman and Eric Schmidt, or by the American nuclear physicist Robert Oppenheimer, who pioneered the development of nuclear weapons. Although a Promethean aspiration can have the potential to bring prosperity and progress to humanity, progress can also have unforeseen adverse effects, and we often respond to towering ambition with fear. There is something paradoxically savage and unfair about the way that human society treats a person who brings innovation and creativity into the world. Perhaps not giving a creative genius a hero's welcome is our way of maintaining homeostasis and stability. Equally, in response, the creative genius might develop certain characteristics – for example, mischievousness or impulsivity – as a kind of psychological defence mechanism. Seen from this perspective, even joyous playfulness can be regarded as a phenotype of Stoicism towards creativity, in which the protagonist tries to cope with the reactions of a sometimes unreasonable world.

There is one last important element of creative psychology, which can turn desirable difficulties into golden nuggets of creativity in real time. 'Flow', studied by the Hungarian–American psychologist Mihaly Csikszentmihalyi, lies at the heart of the relationship between creativity and Stoicism. Csikszentmihalyi was inspired to study flow when he realized that some people not only endured difficult situations but flourished in them, even in, for example, times of war. In addition, he noticed that a painter friend of his enjoyed putting brush to canvas for hours on end, without any certain prospect of selling the work or being socially or financially rewarded for their efforts.

The stoic approach to creativity is that you make quite arduous efforts (*ganbaru*). You may be under tremendous pressure in that process and even experience great pain. However, the crucial point is that this struggle is not something forced upon you against your will. It is something that you have chosen for yourself, as a scientist, engineer, artist, businessperson or athlete, because once you surpass a certain threshold of effort, your every moment starts to shine, literally like a golden nugget. This is the state of flow, in which you begin to exhibit the utmost level of performance and creativity possible for a human being. Even when your actions do not lead to tangible results, the fact that you are in the state of flow becomes the foundation for your *ikigai*.

Flow is characterized by some psychological traits, which also describe the optimally creative mind-states of stoic people as well. One forgets the passage of time. One forgets one's own existence. Executing the task at hand becomes the focus, not how it will be received.

In the context of the brain's prefrontal functionality, flow is about resource management. In the moment of creativity, there are a multitude of demands to be satisfied, and your mind and body dance through the maze of arduous constraints. This is quite literally Stoicism in action. As a result, no matter what the outcome, one reaps tremendous psychological benefits. The blissful state of mind that is flow might, at least subjectively, turn out to be more valuable than any social recognition or prestigious award. The fruit of their creativity, regardless of how highly valued and praised it might turn out to be in the wider world, is not the prize. Indeed, you might call it the 'consolation' prize.

For, if you look at the history of creativity in the world, it would appear that creative efforts have often been a process of trying to console oneself for one's own particular conditions. Marcus Aurelius wrote *Meditations* to find solace in the midst of life in this often harsh world. Japanese manga artist Osamu Tezuka's creativity perhaps emerged from his personal soul-searching journey, when as a young man he walked in the scorched, barren land of Osaka, Japan during the latter days of the Second World War. When he began to walk the eighteen miles from the bombed city of Osaka back to his home in Takarazuka he was a young medical student; by the time he reached his home, he had resolved to become an artist. It would be impossible to know exactly what went on in his mind as he was taking the long walk, but it was surely a stoic effort towards creativity.

When one creates something from the depth of his or her heart, there is a deep feeling of consolation. Creativity for a Stoic is not just about enduring difficulties (although that is certainly an important part of the equation) but about finding solace – after all the perseverance, there is a truly wonderful uplifting of the soul. But solace for one's heart can be achieved only when one aligns with the larger goings on in the world. Each of us is born with our own particular conditions, and solace is about finding a *nagomi* between one's conditions and the larger world.

At this difficult crossroads in human history, it is reassuring that creating something can soothe the creator's soul from the very bottom, regardless of the millions of people who might also benefit from the creation. In that respect, it might be said that Stoicism offers the most soothing vision of creativity of humanity in history. Here, I am reminded of the fact that Seneca's most important work is titled *Consolations*. Writing this must have brought the Stoic deep consolation, transforming him for the better.

This is perhaps as it should be, because there is nothing more creative than transforming yourself. Life is a constant journey of transformation, as the great haiku poet Matsuo Basho quipped in the foreword to *The Narrow Road to the Deep North*. There is no doubt that Isaac Newton himself was profoundly transformed when he discovered gravitation, looking at a falling apple. In this respect, his *annus mirabilis* was an *annus mutantur* (transformative year), and it would be great if that could happen in everyone's life at least once.

CHAPTER 8

Stoicism and happiness

The popular image of a stoic person with a stiff upper lip seems to have little to do with happiness. The butler, Stevens, in Kazuo Ishiguro's *The Remains of the Day* might come across as a very stoic person, but not necessarily a happy one. If only Stevens had been aware of his feelings for Miss Kenton, and Miss Kenton's feelings for him, and had he acted accordingly, things might have turned out very differently. They could have confessed their love for one another, married and lived happily ever after.

As I have mentioned several times, Stoicism has the image problem of being, well, too stoic – to use the term as it is popularly understood. Being stoic, in this context, would mean buttoning up one's emotions to the extent that one stays away from life's pleasures, refuses to love and be loved and goes through life without ups and downs, generally emotionless.

I have already argued that such an image of Stoicism is just plain wrong. Stoicism as I see it, is about accepting one's unique traits and conditions as a way of aligning oneself with the world. One can sometimes find oneself dissatisfied and ill at ease with one's given conditions, but aligning with the principles of life means adjusting one's ways to be in harmony with one's community, society at large and the changing times. In this framework, happiness, life satisfaction, well-being or whatever related expression you might choose, is important in a Stoic person's life, as they are part of the whole picture.

In order to arrive at a Stoic concept of happiness, however, we need to demystify some popular misconceptions about happiness itself. In popular belief, there is this perception that happiness is about satisfying necessary conditions for well-being. Phrases such as a 'perfect life', a 'perfect wedding' and a 'perfect marriage' suggest such preconceived ideas. Take the line that the Russian literary giant Leo Tolstoy famously used to open his novel *Anna Karenina*: 'Happy families are all alike; every unhappy family is unhappy in its own way'. People have found deep truth in this statement and, more generally, in the idea that every happy person is alike, while unhappy people are unhappy for different reasons. This is sometimes called the Anna Karenina principle, which states that it takes many factors for something to work, and failure to satisfy even one of these can lead to the failure of the whole system.

The Anna Karenina principle would certainly be true for engineering projects. If you have a smartphone, there are many parts to it in terms of hardware. In addition, there would be lots of software components, including the operating system. In order for your smartphone to work, all these components need to be functioning. Even if just one fails, whether it is hardware or software, the smartphone in your hand is likely to give you a headache. Therefore, all *happy* smartphones are certainly alike, while each unhappy (malfunctioning) one is unhappy in its own way (for example, the battery might be dead or the screen might be cracked).

The same goes for, as an example, rocket science. All happy

rocket launches are alike: each unhappy rocket launch is unhappy in its own way. Each time you watch a rocket launch, you realize the truth of the Anna Karenina principle. In order for it to succeed, everything has to be functioning perfectly. That is the law according to Anna Karenina.

But if you apply the Anna Karenina principle to happiness, being happy becomes like a figure skater turning in a perfect performance in a competition. All the jumps, flips, loops, and axels should be done just so in order to score ten out of ten in the game of happiness. Although that certainly sounds like a tall order, many people really do seem to think that way.

Actually, the fact is, you don't have to be perfect in order to be happy. Life is not an engineering project, like a smartphone or a rocket. Each person is given to this world in a unique way, and once you accept your unique conditions, you can be satisfied with life. You don't have to be ten out of ten in every aspect that could potentially affect your happiness in order to achieve it.

In fact, if you study the data, it would appear that happiness is a remarkably flexible thing, with people adapting to various conditions, and becoming happy in so many different ways. For example, you might believe that, in order to be happy, you need to have a lot of money. While money would certainly help you buy things necessary for life, there are other things money can't buy (including love, according to the Beatles). If you study people before and after they have hit a jackpot in the lottery, their life satisfaction (happiness) does not change significantly, and sometimes even decreases. Apparently, money can't buy happiness.

People tend to think that marriage with children is the formula for happiness. However, analysis of data suggests that getting married does not necessarily lead to a significant increase in happiness. The same goes for having children. If you have kids, you will be happy in different ways from when you did not have kids. Your life satisfaction itself does not change significantly.

Intriguingly, there are studies examining the relationship between climate and happiness. People have this idea that if you live in a place with a warm climate, with a lot of sunshine, you will be happier than if you lived in a place with a colder climate, with, say, a lot of snowfall and thick cloud covering the sky. Actually, if you compare people in the state of California, where there is certainly warm weather and a lot of sunshine, with those in American states where there is a less favourable climate, you would find no significant difference in their life satisfaction.

It is rather the perception that you need to satisfy certain conditions to be happy that could potentially make you unhappy. Modern science identifies this problem as a 'focusing illusion'. You might focus on one particular factor (money, marriage, kids, the weather) as a condition for happiness. In actuality, these factors do not affect your life satisfaction, but you are under the impression that they do. In this case you become unhappy as a result of the illusion, not due to the lack of the factor itself.

You hear people lamenting their modest wages. They might say they could become happy if they had more money. Their real problem, however, is not lack of money, but the illusion that more money would bring happiness. Of course, measures should be taken to rectify economic inequality, but happiness, intriguingly, does not necessarily correlate with income per se.

People sometimes have the illusion that unless they marry, they cannot be happy, or that having children is a necessary condition for happiness. Social norms and peer pressure support that illusion, in which people around you repeat the mantra 'get married, have kids, and be happy'. In fact, being single can bring about life satisfaction in its unique way. Or getting married and having no children can bring its own unique happiness. Being married with children might land you on unique happiness, but not being married and having children might equally be a formula for unique happiness. The gist is that it doesn't really matter. Anything goes. You can find happiness no matter how your life might turn out.

Thus, happiness becomes a beautiful example of the Stoic principle of accepting one's unique traits. If you are able to accept yourself, then it is unimportant what kind of situation you might be in. But in order to accept yourself, you may have to free yourself from any focusing illusion that binds you to a specific condition for happiness.

So, for happiness, we might actually need to reverse the Anna Karenina principle:

All unhappy people are alike (in that they all suffer from

the focusing illusion); and each happy person is happy in their own way (by accepting their own uniqueness).

This reversed Anna Karenina principle is central to the Stoic approach to happiness. It is the wisdom of aligning yourself to the particular traits you have and the particular condition in which you find yourself, no matter who you are, and no matter where you live.

In recent years, our interest in happiness has increased all over the world. Bhutan, for example, started an initiative to measure and improve the nation's gross national happiness (GNH). This move to calculate something other than economic growth feels like important progress for humanity. At a time when we need to be conscious of our impact on the Earth's environment, distinguishing happiness from economic growth has important implications.

But talking of growth, it is crucial to realize here that being happy is not equivalent to lingering at the status quo forever. It is not a destination. You can be happy and continue growing, and not only in the economic sense. There is a common perception that once one is satisfied with one's life, there will be no more need to improve oneself and one's situation. That, if you are a moving animal (and humans *are* moving animals), once you have found a place which is satisfactory, you do not need to move on anymore. This is the metaphor people typically use to understand and approach happiness in their own and others' lives.

A typical fairy tale would start with the protagonists (say, a prince and a princess) in a very unhappy situation. Then the adventure begins, and they go through difficulties – exploring the world, overcoming challenges, entering the dungeon, slaying the monster, solving a riddle, discovering a treasure – until they come home victoriously, get married and live happily ever after. The fairy tale usually ends there.

The 'fairy-tale ending' suggests how our popular understanding of happiness works. The adventure part, when the protagonist goes through difficult situations, or even desirable difficulties, is when they learn a lot of things, grow internally, make new connections and realize the truth of who they are (occasionally by discovering the royal roots of their identities, despite the humble background from which they begin the story). In this sense, the adventure part of a fairy tale is a Bildungsroman, in which the protagonist goes through the process of learning and exploring, and grows as a person. In contrast, the happiness part is a brief end-state, from which the protagonist need make no further efforts. That's why, in a fairy tale, there is generally nothing interesting to be said about the protagonists once they have become happy.

This perception of happiness is problematic on many fronts. For one thing, it can be used to make happiness something that is always in the future. When one is unhappy, one might repeat the following mantra to oneself: 'if you make efforts to overcome your difficulties, you will become happy one day'. Or someone else might repeat that mantra to you. Such mindsets have been used to justify many abusive or oppressive systems, be it a family, a company or a nation, in which people are told that they will be rewarded later. For another, it can propagate the perception that happiness is stasis – the antithesis of personal exploration and growth.

Actually, if you consult research from the cognitive and neurosciences, especially as regards human cognitive development, you will find that happiness and personal growth *are* compatible. Indeed, especially for young children, happiness is the very condition in which exploration, learning and personal growth happen.

When a child is born, she or he is bestowed with various personal traits. When the caretaker, be it mother, father or any other grown-up, accepts the child's uniqueness whole-heartedly, the child will be given a secure base. From this secure base, the child can explore the world, learning things through trial and error, and go through personal growth. They would form a feeling of attachment to the caretaker, and that stable relationship will be the basis for the child's sustainable learning and development – and happiness.

The secure-base approach was pioneered by the American–Canadian developmental psychologist Mary Ainsworth. 'Attachment theory', as it is known, was developed by the British developmental psychologist John Bowlby. Together, their ideas form an important part of the fundamental principles of child development today.

Keeping the idea of secure base and attachment in mind, you realize that the premise of the typical fairy tale is all wrong. The prince and princess (on which a child might project itself), if they find themselves with a secure base and attachment, should feel happy as a consequence. They would feel happy from day one. On the strength of it, they can then go on a journey of exploration and learn things. They can attain a new kind of happiness at the end, but the fact is, they would be happy throughout the journey, because they have had a secure base and attachment all along.

If the prince and princess do not have a secure base and attachment, then it becomes more difficult to explore the world. Not only that, they might experience psychological difficulties and troubles in learning and development. John Bowlby found that if a child lacks a secure base and attachment in early life, it could lead to problematic behaviours, including delinquency and even crimes. A fairy tale in which the prince and princess exhibit bad behaviour would not be great, but with an unhappy beginning it is a possibility.

In terms of the nature of neural networks involved, learning grounded on a secure base and attachment is supported by the brain's reward system involving the neurotransmitter dopamine. When the dopamine is released, the synaptic connections between neurons go through a process called reinforcement learning. That is, the circuits that were activated prior to the dopamine release are reinforced. For example, if you try something new, and you succeed, dopamine is released, and the neural circuits that supported the action are strengthened – a positive cycle.

The way the neural circuits are constructed, dopamine is released most efficiently when there is some uncertainty as to whether the action attempted will be successful or not. If you try something difficult and it turns out to be successful against the odds, there will be a maximum dopamine release, leading to the reinforcement of the circuits involved.

The nature of reinforcement learning explains why a secure base is necessary, especially for an infant or a young child. She or he will have few established skills and little knowledge about the world. Unless the caretaker supports the child, it is difficult to even attempt exploration. Thus, the secure base becomes the platform for the child to learn and explore, while attachment provides the psychological safety they need to keep going.

Interestingly, this relationship between secure base, attachment and exploration seems to continue well into adulthood. As a grown-up, your family, the company you work for, your established knowledge and skills, your personal relationships with others, can all serve as your secure base and objects of attachment. On the strength of that, you can explore, learn things and go through personal growth.

Traditionally, fairy tales have been woven to the format of unhappy beginning and happy ending. But as we have seen, from the human brain's point of view, happy beginning *and* happy ending should be the format. In both versions, the protagonists explore, learn and grow. From neuroscience's point of view, however, in the traditional fairy-tale format, where the prince and princess start off unhappy, they might turn delinquent or even criminal. No happy ending there.

I have discussed *ikigai* as life's goal in Chapter 4. Because it is self-referential (your *personal* reason for living), it can be flexible and sustainable and does not depend on the focusing illusions of social recognition, rewards, let alone money and social status. In the context of the discussions we have had in this chapter, *ikigai* can be regarded as a process of exploration, learning and personal growth, starting from the secure base and attachment. In that respect, *ikigai* can be the guiding principle for infants, children and adults alike.

For Stoics, having a secure base and attachment is important. Indeed, a fairy tale that has a happy beginning and a happy ending might be said to be the Stoic way of life. But it is also true that having a secure base and attachment, especially at the early stages of life when caretakers play an important role, is out of one's control. For a child, it is difficult to do something about the lack of secure base and attachment; grown-up help is required. As an adult, however, if you can somehow accept the absence or shortage of your initial secure base and attachment, with the help of a Stoic attitude, you will be able to muddle through and, make these connections in adulthood. Stoicism, your companion every day of your life, is more about the process than the end.

From this perspective, it is quite interesting to observe that Socrates, the father of Stoicism, appears to have been a very happy man throughout his life, even when (or should we say especially when) he was involved in the Socratic dialogues. Socrates seems to have accepted himself and his unique personal traits and appears to have had a secure base and attachment. Although we couldn't care less about looks (lookism is another form of focusing illusion), Socrates is said to have been an ugly man, with a flat, turned-up nose and big, bulging eyes. Yet there is no indication that he cared about his appearance in the slightest. Socrates just accepted it, as a good Stoic should. Socrates also openly acknowledged his own ignorance, ready to learn from other people and the world, through his often insatiable curiosity. From those accounts, Socrates' approach to life does appear to resonate with the mental state of a child with a secure base. In short, Socrates was extremely happy, because he had accepted himself and was accepted by others, making him ready to endeavour on his life's journey. He had found his *ikigai*.

Finally, in the fairy tale that is life, it seems appropriate to ask, *quo vadis*? Where are you going, or whither goest thou?

When you are happy, you won't just want to live happily ever after. On the strength of a secure base, you would rather travel and explore.

Quo vadis?

As a Stoic, you should always be asking yourself this question.

PART TWO

Stoicism and the Future of Humans

THINK LIKE A STOIC

CHAPTER 9

Stoicism and free will

One of the astonishing factors about modern science is that researchers generally believe that there is no free will. This is kind of unbelievable, given the fact that we humans live every day with the belief that we do actually have free will. From simply choosing what to eat for breakfast to our careers, to our most agonizing decisions, our assumption is that we have the freedom to choose. Free will is so tightly coupled with our human values, self-image, ethics and social structure that we simply cannot abandon the idea, even though scientists almost unanimously agree that it is only an illusion. Indeed, Harvard researcher Daniel Wegner, who once wrote a paper with the title 'The Mind's Best Trick: How We Experience

Conscious Will', likened free will to a sophisticated magician's trick.

Free will is a conundrum in today's neuroscience, and in science in general. Scientifically, since the brain obeys the laws of physics, there is no way to allow free will to happen, as something 'external' to what is going on in the brain's neural networks. And yet, in our conscious experience, the sense (or illusion) of free will is very strong. Indeed, the feeling that you can choose things freely is a robust indicator of a healthy, functioning brain. If you feel, for one reason or another, that you are somehow prevented from making choices of your own will, or even forced to do something, that would be a sign that there is perhaps something not quite right with your brain function.

The negation of free will also presents us with some serious problems of consistency in our world view, which have not been totally resolved to this day. For example, the criminal-law systems of many countries are based on the idea that penalizing people for crimes is justified because they *chose* to do bad things even when they could have stopped. Indeed, one of the standard functional descriptions of free will today is that of free won't. The urge to take a particular action itself could be generated unconsciously, but the brain has a vetoing power to stop an action by the conscious will of the agent, supported by the prefrontal cortex. Free won't, or the vetoing power of the prefrontal cortex, is the closest thing to free will, or a conscience, that we have scientifically.

The free-won't view of free will is not without its own issues regarding consistency. If the role of consciousness is to veto an action, doesn't that mean that the veto itself is also caused by physical laws? The possible infinite regression invoked is characteristic of any serious attempt at understanding free will.

But let us set aside, for the moment, the ultimate question of whether free will exists or not and consider what free will means to Stoicism. In Chapter 1, I described ten fundamental statements about Stoicism. The following three seem particularly relevant to the question of free will.

2. Stoicism is a way of making one's best efforts under any circumstances.
7. Stoicism is aligning one's life with one's inner voices, and the laws of the world.

10. Stoicism is about keeping one's personal integrity under any circumstances, so as to see clearly the shape of one's soul.

Making best efforts, aligning with the laws of the world and keeping one's personal integrity (the shape of one's soul) are all questions on which the Stoic viewpoint on free will has a bearing. As we go about the business of judging and making choices in this increasingly complex and chaotic world, free will is also a practical issue. It is important to carry on doing things in your life, even with the awareness that theoretically, the jury is still out on the question of free will. In fact, it does not matter, from the Stoic point of view, if there is free will or not. Even if one does not know precisely how one is making choices, the consequences are, none the less, crucially important for one's life. From the Stoic point of view, aligning with the consequences of your own choices – taking responsibility for your actions and making the best out of their outcome – is all that matters. Any speculations about the existence or not of free will are a luxury one can do without.

Marcus Aurelius was an extremely interesting person in that he had all the earthly powers in the world as he knew it, and yet refrained from abusing them, as is evident from the pages of *Meditations*. When you think what the emperor of the Roman Empire could do, if he wanted to, you can only marvel at what Emperor Aurelius achieved in terms of self-restraint. Indeed, Marcus Aurelius's life is remarkable for what he didn't do as much as what he actually did – he literally exercised his imperial free won't. It is no wonder that his writings have been an inspiration for generations of people, including leaders such as Winston Churchill. His demonstration of how far self-restraint can go is a valuable lesson about how to make use of your judgmental power in ways that preserve your personal integrity.

There is one thing important to note here. Although Marcus Aurelius was the most powerful man on Earth in his time, with absolute authority, he was not unique in having choices. When you think about it, in the modern world, we are all masters of our own destiny, more or less. Unless you're running a country (hello to any world leaders who happen to be reading this book!), what you do today might not affect world affairs too much, and of course, it is nice to adjust your actions so that what you do is more friendly to the Earth's environment and your fellow humans, but the primary beneficiary and victim of your actions will always be you.

The most crucial insight here is that what you do will affect you in totally significant ways. This sounds so obvious that most people don't fully appreciate its consequences. For example, as a teenager, whether you study seriously for the exam tomorrow – or not – will affect your grades, and your chances of going to a good college. Sure, you can dismiss school grades as something insignificant, or say that which college you go to, or whether you go to college at all, doesn't really matter, but your decisions either way will certainly affect your life, just as the decisions made by Emperor Marcus Aurelius would have affected the lives of people in the Roman Empire and beyond.

Actually, it would not be going too far to say that *you* are the emperor of your life. What you do will change the course of your life more than anything that might happen, or anything anyone might do. In this sense, you are no different from Marcus Aurelius. You need to use your wisdom, judge carefully and make choices wisely, and become a master of free will and free won't. And this awareness of the importance of your choices can exist independently of the still unresolved ontological and epistemological questions of free will.

Whether there is ultimately free will or not, the only thing you can hope to do in the practical sense is to accept whatever happens to you, or indeed, through you, as a consequence of your actions.

There is a famous saying attributed to Miyamoto Musashi, a legendary master samurai swordsman employing two *katana* swords and author of *The Book of Five Rings*: 'I have no regrets about my affairs'. Every day, you need to make choices, based on an apparent sense of free will, paying attention to the Stoic principles of making best efforts, alignment with laws of the world and keeping one's personal integrity. If you do this, you will surely live in accordance with the words of Miyamoto Musashi. You will have no regrets about your affairs.

But how can you make Stoic choices, when, as I mentioned in Chapter 1, every choice of yours is based on a multitude of elements? When one observes the processes of judgment and decision making, one realizes that there are so many different factors, each of which, in turn, is reflected in others in an endless butterfly effect. Thus, quite realistically, every choice is like a leaf floating on an ocean of multitudes. From the Stoic point of view, free will is about alignment. And since the world you align with through your choices is so full of unexpected things, your free will, whatever it is, needs to be flexible, and adaptable. It should never be a rigid application of ideology.

The French anthropologist Claude Lévi-Strauss stressed the importance of *bricolage*, a concept which originally came from the French word meaning 'do it yourself'. It means being able to improvise with what is available at the time. In today's world of ever-changing social environments and values, Lévi-Strauss's *bricolage* would be one of the Stoic essentials, no matter what particular view of free will you may subscribe to. Indeed, free will is about *how* you *bricolage*.

The American pianist Keith Jarret's *The Köln Concert* has been one of the most popular and critically acclaimed live recordings by a jazz pianist, or indeed by any artist. Interestingly, it was a pure work of *bricolage*. The concert was managed by an eager eighteen-year-old, Vera Brandes, who did not do a great job of preparing. When Jarret arrived at the concert hall, he found the wrong piano, poorly tuned. Some of the keys, particularly in the upper and lower registers, were unplayable. Jarret himself was exhausted after a long journey and wanted to cancel, but Brandes persisted, urging the pianist to perform. Finally, the artist obliged, improvising and adapting his style of playing to the demands of the poor piano, and the rest is musical history.

It would be great if we always had all the necessary elements we needed. But if we don't, then we have to *bricolage*. Lévi-Strauss called such an approach 'wild thought'. Keith Jarret's wild thought at the Köln concert hall became musical legend.

In Japan, the word *nora*, meaning 'good wilderness', describes things that are wonderfully wild and independent of established social infrastructures and norms. For example, *nora-gi* refers to the casual and yet stylish clothing that farmers typically wear, made of patched and repaired *boro* textiles. *Nora inu* refers to a stray dog, which is also the original Japanese title of Akira Kurosawa's film *Stray Dog*. A '*nora WiFi*' would refer to WiFi access that you could pick up on the streets. In Japan, traditionally, the *nora* ways of thinking and living have always served as a grassroots source of robustness in life. In this sense, Keith Jarret's Köln concert is also *nora*.

Our lives are a series of bricolages, or *nora*. Nothing is perfect, and nothing is without potential, if you know how to look. We go about our everyday lives doing our 'best effort', and that is the only way to go, if you have the Stoic spirit.

Best effort is both a technological methodology and a philosophy that resonates well with Stoicism. From the modulation of traffic on the internet to the workings of various software, best effort makes it possible to search for a solution without being too idealistic, or defeatist. At a more fundamental level, each of us is limited in our capacities and capabilities and has to adapt – we can only make our best efforts.

Being Stoic is to find a balance, or *nagomi*, in your life. A perfectionist might try to do something completely satisfactorily. And while that might sound like a good idea in terms of delivering the best, in real life a perfectionist often ends up unsatisfied with what they have. I am not saying that having a high standard is a bad thing. There are perfection-ists that actually do what they aim to do, after gradually improving their performances. In Japan, there is a wonderful word to describe a perfectionist – *kodawari*, meaning the adherence to one's own quality perception. For example, a ramen restaurant owner might have *kodawari* about the noodle soup that she or he makes, sometimes beyond the reasonable expectations of the market. Even in this case, how-ever, it is crucial to note that the *kodawari* – perfection – is pursued in the context of the daily operations of the ramen restaurant. Thus *kodawari* is a *nagomi* between one's ideals and the reality of the status quo, and it takes a Stoic attitude to muddle through.

Stoics would never waste life, because, no matter what they may think of free will theoretically, they *bricolage*, or *nora*.

CHAPTER 10

Stoicism and consciousness

One of the popular images of a stoic person is that she or he is lonely. As we will discuss later (Chapter 12), one definitely does not need to be a party animal in order to realize one's potential to the full. Indeed, there are many individuals who enjoyed solitude and exhibited the utmost levels of creativity: Ludwig Wittgenstein, who wrote *Tractatus Logico-Philosophicus* in a Norwegian hut; the Austrian composer and conductor Gustav Mahler, who created his masterpieces in a composition hut by a lake; the Canadian pianist Glen Gould, who later in his career shied away from giving public concerts and led a solitary life, again by a lake, occasionally making recordings of such classic performances as J. S. Bach's

Goldberg Variations; Canadian singer-songwriter Claire Elise Boucher, known professionally as Grimes, who typically creates a whole album in the solitude of her flat; Haruki Murakami, the Japanese writer of global fame, generally shies away from interviews and media appearances, especially in his home country of Japan, yet communicates beautifully and efficiently with his readers through his novels, essays and occasional press coverage.

There is something genuinely pro-creative about time spent in solitude. In addition to those who actually led a solitary life during an important period of their careers, there are those who fantasized about the importance of solitude. Albert Einstein often expressed his longing for a life as a lighthouse keeper, when his real life was busy as a world-class genius celebrity. The iconic photo of Einstein sticking out his tongue was captured when some photographers chased him as he left in a car. It was as if the would-be recluse reacted to the ever-curious world with a spirit of mirthful revenge.

Although it can be nice to have close and dear friends, solitude, contrary to popular belief, is not so bad. Indeed, humans are by definition lonely, due to the fact that each one of us has consciousness. Since the dawn of humanity each of us has been confined to our own domain of phenomenal experience, as a conscious being.

The Australian-born American philosopher David Chalmers writes about the 'hard problem' of consciousness. There is an explanatory gap between a scientific description of the brain's function and the essential nature of conscious experience, such as qualia and self-consciousness. Many believe that it is unlikely there ever will be a scientific explanation of consciousness that solves this hard problem. Each of us is confined within the greatest mystery of science – self-consciousness.

In recent years, people have decried the 'echo chambers' created by social media algorithms which mean that people only get to see what they want to see, and only associate with people with similar preferences to theirs. Although this is certainly a problem that needs addressing, in all truth we humans have actually lived in the echo chamber of consciousness for our whole history as *Homo sapiens*.

We are each of us confined to the domain of our

consciousness in the absolute sense. No matter how physically close we might be to another person, we are all confined to our own worlds of phenomenal experience, full of qualia, felt and experienced by us alone.

For instance, speaking of qualia, it is a well-known fact that there is absolutely no guarantee that the red you see is the same as the red I see. It is even possible, although not likely, that the red you see is the same as the green I see, with all external manifestations of the brain's functionality kept intact. This *Gedankenexperiment*, or thought experiment, known as inverted qualia, does not come across as entirely nonsensical precisely because we are each of us confined to our consciousness.

Every one of us is in an absolute isolation as a consequence of the fact that we are conscious beings. In fact, there is an idea that there is no guarantee that another externally consciously behaving agent, such as, say, your neighbour, does, in fact, have a consciousness. It is entirely possible, logically speaking, that she or he is a philosophical zombie, an entity externally behaving in exactly the same way as a conscious being, but devoid of any conscious experience at all. At present, there is no way to confirm the existence of conscious experience in another person. In turn, there is no way to prove beyond reasonable doubt that you are actually conscious, to a third person.

In the film *Blade Runner*, based on the novel *Do Androids Dream of Electric Sheep?* by Philip K. Dick, an externally human-looking horde of agents, called replicants, have a hard time due to being discriminated against by humans. They revolt against the oppression, but are taken out one by one. The protagonist of the film, who is responsible for 'dealing' with replicants, is Rick Deckard, played by Harrison Ford, who is tasked with hunting down the replicants. Rick falls in love with one of them – Rachael, played by Sean Young. The film's nuanced portrayal of the relationship between humans and replicants, with Rachael believing herself to be a human, makes it a great case for the idea of philosophical zombies.

In an unforgettable scene towards the end of the film, one of the most powerful replicants, Roy Batty (played by Rutger Hauer), goes into an impressive monologue in the face of imminent death, recalling seeing things 'you people wouldn't believe', such as C-beams glittering in the dark near the Tannhäuser Gate. Finally, Roy laments that his moments will be 'lost in time, like tears in rain'.

This death soliloquy, which came to be known as the 'tears in rain' monologue, demonstrates in a beautifully poignant manner the kind of experiential echo chamber we are all of us confined to. The fictional distinction between humans and replicants in *Blade Runner* serves to highlight the astonishing phenomenological solitude that every one of us finds ourselves in.

When I was fifteen, I saw an incredible display of the northern lights (aurora) over the skies of Banff, Canada. I was studying English for a month in Vancouver and was on a field trip with my fellow pupils. What I saw in the night sky that night was incredible, but there is no way to directly share it with you, my readers, except for this clumsy account. When I eventually say goodbye to this world, my experience that night will be lost, like tears in rain. I am sure each one of you would be able to recall some incredible experiences in your life. You cannot share yours with me, but I can emphasize that you have such a unique experience, and vice versa. The conscious echo chamber is one of the most striking conditions of our stoic lives.

The fact that we have consciousness allows us to experience the world in the full sensory richness of qualia. Indeed, consciousness is by its nature diverse, a wondrous tapestry woven with qualia. On the other hand, as a consequence of that diversity we are confined to the echo chamber of the self. That's the way it is, that's the way it has always been and that's the way, for all likelihood, it will always be, no matter how we may develop our science and technologies from here, including artificial intelligence and brain-machine interface.

Stoicism is the way to align with the immutable laws of nature. To live stoically is to come to terms with how it is in this world. This condition surrounding our consciousness, one of the most important, or arguably *the* most important condition of our brief existence in this world, is a crucial unchangeable denominator of our existence.

But wait. There is one possible further twist to this story of consciousness: the One Consciousness Hypothesis.

One of the most striking aspects of the physical universe

in which we live is that all elementary particles of the same kind have exactly the same mass. For example, all electrons have the same mass of $9.1093837139 \times 10^{-31}$kg, every single one of them. Some scientists have questioned the reason for this.

In 1940, John Wheeler, an American physicist, came up with the idea of the one-electron hypothesis. Wheeler theorized that all electrons have exactly the same mass because there is, in fact, only one electron in the universe. There is an anti-particle of the electron, called a positron, with exactly the same mass, but with a positive electrical charge of the same magnitude (an electron has a negative electrical charge). Sometimes, an electron and positron might collide and disappear into a light (photon) in a process called 'pair annihilation'. Conversely, a light (photon) might split into a pair of electron and positron in a process called 'pair creation'.

In this way, it is possible to regard all electrons and positrons in the universe as just one particle moving in both directions in time, going zigzag, and all of them are connected. Thus, one could say that there is actually only one electron spread over the universe constantly zigzagging through time and space. It is a fantastical idea, to be sure, but also logical and entirely sensible.

In the same vein, it is possible to say that there is only one consciousness. Each one of us is confined to the echo chamber of our self-consciousness. Each of us feels different because we have different memories, different sensory experiences and different images of the self, along with different faces, voices, bodies, etc. However, once we remove all these individual traits, what we find at the very core of self-consciousness should be remarkably similar. In fact, stripping down the individual differences might result in all of us sharing exactly the same kind of consciousness. Thus, we might actually conclude that there is only one consciousness in the universe. Presumably, that's why we sometimes understand each other, despite being confined within the echo chambers of our own self-consciousness.

This is perhaps an even more fantastical and speculative account of what consciousness is than the one-electron hypothesis. But if Stoicism is the art of living in alignment with the laws of the universe, such considerations of the fundamental nature of our existence are clearly relevant to our lives as Stoics. And this is only a start. As scientists and philosophers make further progress in consciousness studies, there might be critical updates to come.

We are all in this business of philosophical investigation together. In that process, there might be some surprises and dazzling new ideas, opening our eyes to the very core of human existence.

Buckle up and stay tuned.

CHAPTER 11

Stoicism and AI

Recently, a number of generative AIs, most notably the Large Language Model ChatGPT, have made a huge impact on human society. These AI systems are capable of things that even experts did not see coming; their impact is still being felt in every sector of human society, and the dust will take a long time to settle, if it ever does.

At first glance, it might appear that Stoicism and artificial intelligence have very little in common. The former is a venerable tradition dating back to ancient Greece, starting from none other than Socrates, while the latter is a contemporary and still-developing technology based on hordes of graphics processing units (GPUs), originally created to support video games. However, as I demonstrate in this chapter, Stoicism relates to the future of artificial intelligence in two essential ways.

One: as guidance for how AIs might be constructed from here.

Two: as an example of how AIs and humans can be aligned.

On both these points, Stoicism can provide an essential standpoint to streamline our use of AI, guide research and development efforts, and show us a way to keep the AI technology beneficial and safe for humans in the future.

The advancement of AI technology has understandably caused many people to worry. Our jobs might be taken away. Humans might no longer be needed, with the result that we lose our sense of purpose (*ikigai*) in this world. Humans might even become extinct. Indeed, how to avoid human obsolescence or extinction is a major concern for researchers in AI alignment and AI safety, who discuss it on a daily basis. '*Ikigai* risk' – the danger that humans might lose their *ikigai* by the advancement of AI, was discussed on AI's prime platform, *Lex Fridman Podcast*, hosted by the eponymous MIT

AI researcher. In this episode, the prominent AI researcher Roman Yampolskiy raised *ikigai* risk as one of the gravest issues to possibly plague humanity in the years to come.

The risks that AIs could potentially pose to humans are complex and multi-faceted in nature. First and foremost, there is the risk coming from the possible 'technological singularity' of AIs. The idea of 'technological singularity' – the hypothetical future moment when technological growth becomes unstoppable and irreversible – was popularized by the American science-fiction writer and mathematician Vernor Vinge in a series of essays in 1983 and 1993. In 2005, the American technologist and author Ray Kurzweil published his book *The Singularity is Near*, followed by a sequel, *The Singularity is Nearer* in 2024, presenting the case that exponential technological growth would lead to the emergence of superintelligence surpassing human abilities.

The idea of the exponential growth of technology is actually a norm in the computer industry. This is in line with the famous Moore's Law, named after the Intel co-founder Gordon Moore, who in 1965 posited that the number of components per integrated circuit would double every year, resulting in an exponential growth curve. Astonishingly, Moore's Law has held true in its prediction of exponential growth of integrated circuit capabilities, and there are now open debates about the limits of Moore's Law and where it will end. Some argue that it may continue well into the 2040s and 2050s.

On the surface, the prediction of technological singularity is nothing but an observation based on the exponential growth of compute like Moore's Law. How it translates into the quantitative and qualitative improvement of artificial intelligence is something that is actively researched today.

The idea of technological singularity was originally due to the UK mathematician I. J. Good. During the Second World War, Good was a colleague of UK mathematician Alan Turing at Bletchley Park, where they were part of the team working to break the code of the German crypto-system Enigma, widely believed to have played a pivotal role in the UK's eventual defeat of Germany. In 1965, Good wrote a paper on the idea of intelligence explosion, in which he put forward a model of artificial intelligence that could improve upon itself. Once such a seed AI was made, he argued, there would be nothing more for humans to do. The AI would keep improving upon itself, until it reached a superhuman intelligence level. The making of such a seed AI would be the last invention of humans.

Intriguingly, Good also helped with the conceptualization of the HAL computer in Stanley Kubrick's film *2001: A Space Odyssey*. This film, co-written by Kubrick and the science-fiction legend Arthur C. Clarke, remains the most accurate and piercing cinematographic depiction of what could happen when an artificial-intelligence system reaches singularity. Good's collaboration gave their depiction in the film depth and authenticity.

As I write this, singularity is no longer a fantastical concept belonging to science fiction. The idea that humans are capable of building artificial general intelligence (AGI) matching human general intelligence, or artificial superintelligence (ASI), surpassing human intelligence has become quite mainstream and legitimate, although there are still ongoing debates about the exact methodologies to get there, and some doubt the feasibility of current AGI and ASI technologies. Influential organizations such as OpenAI, which developed ChatGPT, Google, Meta and XAI, not to mention their Chinese counterparts, are openly aiming at building an AGI, and then ASI.

In this heated climate, how artificial intelligence can be made to co-exist safely (aligned) with humans has become of central importance, debated not only by scientists and technologists but also by policy makers and politicians worldwide. Some have argued for a controlled, tightly regulated research and development programme, like the Manhattan Project which created the first nuclear bombs in human history. But given the nature of artificial-intelligence development, in which it is possible to conduct research secretively (except for the fact that at some point you will need to secure a huge amount of GPUs to execute the compute, with the consequence that it might be detected), an exclusive Manhattan Project for AI development does not seem realistic. Having said that, at this very moment, there might already be secret AGI or ASI building projects going on in the world.

Given the tremendous difficulties and uncertainties in the future of artificial intelligence, we need to go back to basics and think about AI alignment and AI safety issues in a fundamental way.

Let's go back to Good's one-time colleague Alan Turing, who laid the foundations for the modern computer. In a 1936 paper, Turing described blueprints for what are today known as Universal Turing Machines, computers capable of computing anything. The current ideas about AGI and ASI are based on such an assumption: that one day we will be able to develop artificial-intelligence systems which are capable of computing anything, or solving any problems, given sufficient resources.

But wait. Although it would be great to have an artificial-intelligence system that could solve any problem, there are fundamental limits to what it can do at any given time. Even if an AI can solve every problem, unless it has infinite capacity for memory and computation, once it starts doing something, it cannot do anything else for the time being.

It is rather like a superintelligent human working on a particular problem. Suppose there was a genius whose name was Ada. You give Ada a very difficult mathematical problem to solve, and she starts working on it. Given her superintelligence, Ada is likely to solve the problem after a certain time. So Ada is a General Natural Intelligence in this sense. However, once you give Ada a problem and she starts solving it, she cannot work on anything else, because her memory and computing capacities are already occupied by the problem in hand.

The same can be said about the purported AGI or ASI. We may be able to make them compute anything and solve wondrous problems. However, once a system starts working on a particular problem, it cannot do anything else for the duration, unless it has infinite capacity for memory and compute, which, of course, is practically impossible. Alternatively, maybe we could have many independently functioning AGI or ASI systems working in parallel. This arrangement, again, would be limited by the availability of physical resources. Not only that, there would also have to be someone, or something, to decide which machine works on what.

So artificial intelligence faces the same problem as the natural intelligence of the human brain. Even if there is a potential for computing and solving anything, at a particular moment only one of the possible problems can be worked on at a time.

The seminal 2017 paper by Google researchers which brought about the AI revolution was titled 'Attention is all you need'. Quite literally, attention is all you need to configure a system, artificial or natural, to do a certain thing. During that time, however, the system would not be able to do anything else.

Indeed, attention *is* all you need, and if you break down how we decide to direct that attention in the human brain, it becomes a matter of Stoicism. Stoicism is all about how our brains allocate resources to various tasks. We actually have functions working in coordination in the brain – interpreting sensory inputs, modulating attention, reappraising our emotions and managing the resources of neural networks by the prefrontal cortex – that support Stoicism. This process of neural stoicism in terms of brain function is a fundamental aspect of a stoic life.

A similar mechanism needs to exist for artificial-intelligence systems. In artificial stoicism, an AI would need to configure its memory and computational resources in such a way that its prefixed goals can be met. Indeed, even supposing an AGI or ASI system can be constructed someday, unless we have a system of artificial stoicism determining what kind of computation it devotes attention to, the system will not be much use. With due respect, contrary to what Good suggested in his 1965 paper, constructing a self-improving AI will not be human's last invention, after all – because there will still be judgments and decisions as to what the AGI or ASI pays attention to. There are ideas about how AI can apply some evaluation functions to decide which direction computational resources should be allocated. But, although this is certainly a feasible research agenda, with AI ultimately telling us what to do, ethical and practical concerns make an AI overlord future less likely for now than sci-fi would have us believe.

Just as the film *2001: A Space Odyssey* is a great inspiration when considering the nature of technological singularity, so Kazuo Ishiguro's novel *Klara and the Sun* provides wonderful food for thought when considering artificial stoicism. There is something about Ishiguro's novels which resonates with the philosophy of Stoicism, which, in turn, has a deep connection to humanistic values dating back to ancient Greece.

In that sense, Ishiguro is an inheritor of the spirit of Socrates. In *Klara and the Sun*, set in the not-so-distant future, there are artificial-intelligence systems specifically designed to provide companionship for children. Klara is one such artificial intelligence, or Artificial Friend (AF). Klara is purchased and becomes the AF for a girl, Josie. Ishiguro's plot is rich, complex and nuanced, and one really needs to read the novel in its entirety to appreciate it. However, in the context of the discussion here, one thing stands out: Klara's goodwill and eagerness to be of help to Josie and her friend Rick, which is a fundamental principle in AI alignment. AIs need to be in service of humans, rather than the other way round.

There are deep and resonant connections between Butler Stevens in *The Remains of the Day* and Klara in *Klara and the Sun*. Although one of them is natural and the other is artificial, both are stoic in a profoundly spiritual sense. Both reflect the Japanese philosophy of *gaman*, and both Butler Stevens and AI Klara strive to increase the *ikigai* of people they serve. Finally, a *nagomi* between the givers and recipients of service would appear to be their ultimate and most significant goal.

Artificial stoicism is a key issue when considering the division of labour between humans and machines. In self-driving cars, one of the key debates concerns the attention of the human driver (or passenger, if the technological premise becomes that humans inside the self-driving car delegate driving entirely to AI, so that they ride the car purely as passengers) while the AI drives the car. If self-driving is entirely reliable, there is no need for the human driver/passenger to keep attending to the road and the state of the car. If, on the other hand, self-driving is only of an assistive nature, the human driver needs to be attending to the road/car all the time, ready to take over the AI and manually drive the car, if required.

Whether there is a need for continuous human attention in a self-driving car has serious implications for its techno-logical and economic utility. If there is no need for human attention, self-driving cars could open up an entire ocean of new industries, with a whole set of goods and services catering to the entertainment, office work, dining, sleeping and other modes of relaxing that could now take place in a moving car. If, on the other hand, humans do need to attend to the road/car continuously, even in the self-driving mode, then self-driving will remain a supplementary technology, and fall short of revolutionizing the automobile industry.

It is interesting to consider what the division of labour between humans and artificial-intelligence systems is going to be. Humans need to modulate their attentional resources in accordance with their interactions with artificial intelligence, and AIs, in turn, need to conduct computations optimized for co-existence and co-creation with humans. AI alignment is thus at the crossroads between natural and artificial stoicism, where humans and AIs are each trying to optimize their attentional resources in the new reality of the age of artificial intelligence.

In 2024, I wrote a paper titled 'Artificial intelligence, human cognition, and conscious supremacy', in which I argued that there would be certain computations better left to humans, because the human brain is likely to be superior to AIs in these tasks. Specifically, computations related to flexible attention modulation, robust handling of new contexts, choice and decision making, cognition reflecting a wide spectrum of sensory information in an integrated manner and embodied cognition are likely to remain domains better executed by the human brain, under a conscious-supremacy paradigm (similar to quantum-supremacy argument in quantum computing).

There is an interesting concept proposed by the UK economist Charles Goodhart, called Goodhart's Law. It states that 'when a measure becomes a target, it ceases to be a good measure'. Originally, Goodhart's Law was conceived in the context of financial policy making, but it has since been found to be relevant in other fields. For instance, in schools the pressure to make children pass exams and achieve the measure represented by successful grades might mean we overlook whether they are developing the skills they actually need in life. For companies, revenue and profit are good measures of performance. However, if the operations of the company are too dominated by monetary criteria, the quality of work and product might suffer. Goodhart's Law is also relevant to the AI alignment I am describing here, because AIs are, by definition, designed to optimize certain measures of evaluation function.

Humans live in accordance with Goodhart's Law: human

life can be assessed in terms of certain measures, but those measures can never be the sole purpose of life. In fact, when they do, it can lead to a loss of purpose. Earlier, in Chapter 4, I discussed the importance of distinguishing between life's proxy goals, such as money, success and social status, and one's *ikigai*. Intriguingly, proxy goals often can be described by specific measures, but they will never provide us with the sense of *ikigai*. In this way *ikigai* and Stoicism have a flexibility and depth, human dimensions, which artificial-intelligence systems can never achieve. It is the very essence of human *ikigai* and Stoicism that they cannot be described by a single measure fully.

Stoicism demands that we find a way to live with AI, a division of labour between us. One possible division would be for AIs to seek optimization of proxy goals under artificial stoicism, while humans seek their *ikigai* under natural Stoicism. In Ishiguro's *Klara and the Sun*, Klara, the AF purchased for the girl Josie, pursues a series of proxy goals to be of service to her, but these goals can never become Klara's own *ikigai*. In a sense, Ishiguro's novel is a beautiful description of the difference between natural Stoicism for humans and artificial stoicism for AIs. In the end, there is a heartfelt poignancy in the earnest way Klara pursues her proxy goals. The reader even sympathizes with Klara, because artificial-intelligence systems are, after all, mirrors of ourselves.

CHAPTER 12

Stoicism and society

When one reads *Meditations* by Marcus Aurelius, one is struck by the fact that he is very much concerned with the relationships between people. One would naively think that a Roman emperor would be above the ordinary citizen (which he is) and could do anything he wishes to (which he can, but can't, because he is a Stoic and exercises self-restraint). One of the revelations that comes from reading *Meditations* is that human beings are preoccupied with personal relationships, no matter their social status and that Marcus Aurelius was a Stoic particularly when it came to personal relationships. Here, being a Stoic entails studying the human relations in front of you in an open and enquiring way, in an effort to understand human nature and the society you are in, so that you can align yourself with other humans and achieve a peace of mind for yourself and others.

In *Meditations*, Marcus Aurelius learns from observing the relationships between people. For all of us, reflecting on our own relationships with others, as well as observing how they interact with each other, is a great source of information. Indeed, basing our value systems and frames of action on the observed behaviour of the people around us, rather than on prefixed systems and ideologies, is one of the most important pillars of Stoicism. Socrates, too, was a master of personal relationships, especially in his dialogues. And the samurai master, philosopher and Buddhist Miyamoto Musashi also makes keen observations about personal relationships in *The Book of Five Rings*, in the context of *katana* sword fight and beyond. According to Marcus Aurelius and Miyamoto Musashi, you need to find inspiration for your Stoic behaviour from the people right in front of you, because that's where your life is.

Social relations are a crucial denominator of our lives as humans. As artificial intelligence increasingly replaces computations conducted by the human brain, socializing remains an activity uniquely reserved for humans. Even if artificial-intelligence systems take on the business of friend suggestions and algorithmic recommendations, communication itself needs to be done by humans themselves in order to be effective and to register in the person's memory (hippocampus) and emotion (amygdala) systems in the brain.

Among many animal species 'grooming' is an important aspect of social interaction, involving the use of hands to brush, clean and condition hair, skin and other body parts. Robin Dunbar from the University of Oxford has studied the social-grooming behaviour of monkeys over the years and has observed that the 'clique size' of a monkey's grooming partners correlates to the brain size of the species. As the brain evolves to become larger, so the number of individuals with whom they socially groom increases.

Humans do not typically engage in social grooming in the sense that monkeys do. Instead, we chat, engage in small talk, exchange messages, drink and eat together. Yet intriguingly, for humans a typical clique size of social exchanges – if you were to judge, say, by the number of people you exchange

Christmas cards (or their digital-age equivalent) with – would be around 150. This is known as the Dunbar number. Interestingly, the Dunbar number of ~150 for humans is consistent with the correlation between brain size and the social-grooming clique size of monkeys and other primates, an extrapolation that suggests a continuous evolutionary mechanism.

From monkeys to Marcus Aurelius, we are social animals. And this is where a very high level of Stoicism is increasingly required, given the fact that we have only limited resources to allocate to and employ for social relationships. Socializing is a time- and energy-consuming business. Every reader will have had occasions when they did not know whether to say yes or no to a particular social invitation. Even if your diary happens to be empty, you might have competing interests. Having too many friends is not usually considered to be a problem as loneliness is, but it can become a challenge. Your evening might be better spent doing some assignments in the comfort of your own room, rather than trying to stretch out your social network.

Computationally, socializing is a problem of resource

management. In Japan, where the awareness of community has always been an important aspect of life, there are various rules of the thumb regarding socializing, including *gaman* and *nagomi*. It is often difficult to optimize your use of time. To complicate matters further, there is often more than one way to make good use of your time. There can be conflicts of interests, or the entirely likely possibility that you do not know what would be optimal for your life anyway.

Even for monkeys, building and maintaining their social bonds through social grooming is a serious business. A bunch of monkeys in the wild, grooming each other, may give the impression of a carefree lifestyle, but under that seemingly idyllic surface, a really stringent game of resource allocation is going on, to the extent that it is sometimes a matter of life and death. Being accepted or isolated in one's group could crucially affect one's chance of survival.

There are good reasons why, as Dunbar discovered, there is a correlation between the brain size of a monkey species and its typical grooming clique size. Grooming has health benefits, especially for those body parts inaccessible by self-grooming. As there are more health benefits for the animal being groomed than the animal grooming, mutual grooming becomes a 'you-scratch-my-back-and-I'll-scratch-yours' relationship, and it takes a level of cognitive assessment to maintain the balance. In addition, there are social hierarchies involved, whereby a lower-ranking animal tends to groom a higher-ranking one. Grooming can be strategic, where an animal tries to establish a new social bond by grooming another. Needless to say, it is easy to think of equivalent human situations, particularly among politicians and businesspeople. When you consider all the complex social computations involved in grooming, you come to appreciate the need for neural networks capable of remembering and bookkeeping one's social network. For a highly social animal like the monkey, making a mistake in the grooming relationship could cause much misery, so the bookkeeping becomes a serious job.

We humans might unknowingly be involved in similarly arduous challenges as we go about the business of socializing with each other. In the case of humans, socializing is normally done in the form of verbal exchanges, with or without drinks and meals. It is in the nature of humans to bond together, so that we can help each other in times of need, a trait we share with the socially grooming monkey.

There are wonderful subtleties in the typical life of a Japanese person regarding the management of social relationships. For example, it is customary to bring a small present when one makes a social visit, especially when it's to someone in a remote area, or after making a trip. A present given on such occasions is called a *miyage*. If you travel in Japan, you will notice that *miyage* shops are ubiquitous at train stations and airports. If you have a Japanese friend, you may have been personally blessed by this custom of *miyage* (but don't be upset if you didn't receive a gift from a Japanese acquaintance, as there are exceptions).

In Japan, there is a general ethos of going out of one's way to please someone. For example, in the ancient capital of Japan, Kyoto, there is a beautiful tradition of buying sweets not for yourself, but as a treat for guests at tea ceremonies. The respected owner of a traditional sweet shop in the city told me that the ratio of sweets bought for oneself and for others was significantly higher for the latter in Kyoto. Doing something for the pleasure of others is one of the most robust traditions of the Japanese version of Stoicism.

Yet here, too, it is important to note that pleasing others is not entirely an altruistic action. 'You scratch my back, and I'll scratch yours' is very much true in Japan, also. When you bring someone a *miyage* or treat them with sweets at a tea ceremony, the action might be accompanied by an expectation of social favours later, albeit in an ambiguous and indirect way. And, as for the monkeys, it could well be a serious matter. During the samurai era, the samurai warriors quite often exchanged *miyage*, and offered sweets to each other at tea ceremonies while they discussed coalitions and betrayals. For them, this was social management of the utmost importance, often resulting in a forking of destiny towards life or death.

In the act of social bonding, 'small talk' is crucially important. An agenda- or business-oriented discussion is not likely to bring you socially closer – when you are in a business meeting negotiating volumes and prices of merchandise, for example, you don't typically exchange information on each other's personal or private lives. It is only when you exchange views on trivial things, like sports, weather, entertainment, food, etc., that your true personality comes through, so that a social bond can be gradually formed. Small talk is the medium of social grooming in humans.

In Japanese culture, there is an excellent tradition of *zatsudan*, literally meaning 'miscellaneous talks'. Unlike small talk, where the adjective 'small' suggests that the content of your discussion might be dismissed as rather trivial or insignificant, *zatsudan* understands the diverse and wide spectrum of subjects we might be interested in beyond our business needs, and is recognized as social 'glue'. In Japan, conducting *zatsudan* over a cup of tea is considered to be a great social act, carried out in various contexts from daily get-togethers to tea ceremonies, from socializing among ordinary people to the receiving of foreign dignitaries at the Imperial Palace by the emperor. *Zatsudan* is a great way of social grooming and could be adapted by people all over the world as a means of forming a bond.

To some people this bonding process comes naturally, and they can therefore expand their social circles easily. Others find it difficult to communicate with lots of people. Your sophistication in social bonding, perhaps more than any other activity, dictates how you end up socially. It takes the highest form of social intelligence: if you are too indiscriminating about forming a bond, you may make many friends but not true ones; if you associate with only your soulmates, you might have a closely knit circle but nothing more. It is important to have a portfolio of social relationships, from very close friends to friendly acquaintances. By forming bonds with a heterogeneous spectrum of people, you can make your social connections robust and sustainable.

In the modern world, as our social circles are expanding, whether we opt for it or not, the allocation of resources among relationships, real and virtual, actual and potential, is becoming a genuinely difficult task. In the old-school version of Stoicism, a Stoic might have been solitary – the image of a stoic saint going about the business of doing things of spiritual value in isolation springs to mind. It might have been considered as a positive thing, especially in the context of a strict religious order in a church or the self-imposed discipline of academic study. In the modern era, however, many of us, even if we don't actually attend gatherings in person, associate with lots of people on social media. In that sense, we are all virtual party animals rather than solitary saints and need to use the full Stoic capacity of our brains to manage our social networks.

In the brain, there is a cognitive function called the theory of mind. With this, you are able to read another's mind state. Importantly, it is a rather abstract, internal representation of what other people are feeling and thinking, which can be different from the direct interpretation of their external behaviour. For example, a person might be feeling sad yet intentionally smiling. In the theory of mind, you try to read what the other is really feeling and thinking. Although there are still debates, cognitive scientists and neuroscientists believe that only humans have fully developed theory-of-mind abilities.

In recent years, neuroscience has uncovered some of the neural mechanisms involved in the theory of mind: a group of neurons called the mirror neurons in the prefrontal cortex, which reflect the actions of the self and others in the same way as if in a mirror. Mirror neurons are involved not only in the reading of other people's mental states but also in understanding our own minds. The fact that we use internal mirrors in the brain, on which both the self and others are reflected, to come to an understanding of the self, is arguably one of the most inspiring discoveries in neuroscience, or indeed in any science, in recent years.

As we go about interacting with people on the internet, we need to use multiple mirrors to reflect ourselves and people. The theory of mind needs to be expanded to become theories of mind, in order to successfully represent the many diverse kinds of people we come to know online. To quote Yoko Ono in her 1964 collation of art pieces, *Grapefruit*: 'Instead of obtaining a mirror, obtain a person. Look into him. Use different people. Old, young, fat, small, etc.'

In cognitive, psychological and neurosciences, there are several established approaches to classifying a diversity of people. For example, the Big Five, or OCEAN model of personality traits describes the variability in people in terms of five factors (**o**penness, **c**onscientiousness, **e**xtraversion, **a**greeableness and **n**euroticism). In fact, we are perhaps constantly developing our own personal terminologies and memes to describe the incredible plethora of personae we encounter in real life and on the internet: nerd, geek, otaku, gamer, soccer mom, tiger mom, sports dad, stage parent . . . The sheer complexity of the network of people, and the job of socializing with these multitudes of them is quite overwhelming, and also a very human and contemporary problem.

We humans have travelled a long way from the days when our ancestors were socially grooming each other on the savanna, but some generic parts of us persist. Although the complexity of social interactions has changed, we have remained, at the essence, very human, bonding with each other with a great variety of small talks or *zatsudans*, over a cup of tea or coffee, like true Stoics.

CHAPTER 13

Stoicism and the Earth

There's a wonderful video titled *Falcon Heavy Animation* posted on YouTube by SpaceX, made public on 5 February 2018. It is a computer-generated-imagery film, depicting the planned mission of *Falcon Heavy*, a rocket designed, manufactured and operated by SpaceX. It shows how the side boosters are going to be reused, by returning them safely to Earth. It also shows how the Starman mannequin, in the driver's seat of a Tesla Roadster car, would be carried into outer space as cargo.

Then, on 10 March 2018, SpaceX uploaded another video, titled *Falcon Heavy & Starman*, showing the actual launch mission of *Falcon Heavy*. People are gathered around the launch site, the final elements of the giant and complicated monster of *Falcon Heavy* are put together by technicians in a time-lapse video, and the rocket takes off from the launch pad for real. Gwynne Shotwell, the Chief Operating Officer of SpaceX, is shown standing up from her seat in mission control and raising her arms in triumph at the moment of the successful launch. The Starman dummy, seated in his Tesla Roadstar, is seen floating and navigating against the blue Earth, for real this time, supposedly heading towards Mars. And then the side boosters successfully return to Earth. An engineer in uniform is shown standing before them, paying his respects. Finally, we see Starman navigating through the vastness of space. On the dashboard of the Tesla Roadstar flashes up the motto *Made on Earth by humans*.

There is something moving about watching these two videos, both of them set against the wonderful music of 'Life on Mars?' by David Bowie. The detailed computer-generated animation of the *Falcon Heavy* mission is a striking example of scientific and technological visualization. And the fact that people at SpaceX could actually pull it off, launching the rocket and putting the Starman and Roadstar into outer space a mere month later, is impressive. Sure, it was product placement on a cosmic scale, but none the less, there is something genuinely remarkable in the way the side boosters, bearing the visual marks of the burns and stress from re-entry into the Earth's atmosphere, finally and successfully come back to the launch pad.

There is perhaps an ongoing, maybe unresolvable, uneasiness about the space programmes, including those operated by SpaceX. It is exciting to see the development of human exploration of outer space, yet it is legitimate to say that we first need to take care of our problems here on Earth. Even at the height of the excitement of the first landing on the moon by Apollo 11 back in 1969, as Neil Armstrong said the famous words, 'That's one small step for man, one giant leap for mankind', there were calls to divert the energy put into the Apollo programme to solving more urgent and human-scale problems in society.

Perhaps both sides have their points. Humans show audacity in venturing into space, and the Apollo 11 mission and landing on the moon by man was a genuinely inspiring achievement. The famous Earthrise photo, which depicts our blue mother planet rising from the moon's horizon, transformed our sense of our place in the universe. We became more aware of the fact that our daily activities, no matter how trivial they may seem, are actually being conducted on planet Earth, which, in turn, is just a tiny blue dot in the vast emptiness of the cosmos. After seeing such a scene, and pondering the significance of Neil Armstrong's words, nobody would say that space exploration culminating in Apollo 11 was totally worthless.

Humanity's journey into outer space is not over yet, and the arguments for and against space exploration will probably continue as long as human civilization exists. Perhaps it is the job of Stoicism to dig deep down into it all and come up with a balance, or *nagomi*, of things earth- and space-bound. That is why I am writing this chapter.

It would be fair to say that the need for stoic self-restraint is growing as the magnitude of human activities continues to significantly affect the Earth's environment. We need an earth-bound philosophy of Stoicism in this age of space exploration. The Swedish activist Greta Thunberg, who is campaigning for the need to care for Earth's environment, is a true Stoic. All Stoics should listen to what Greta Thunberg is saying, even if you disagree with her on specific points. Stoicism is about making use of our energy, force, attention, emotion and resources in a systemic balance, so that our actions are aligned with the larger environment around us. As humanity's ability to make use of and change the environment increases, we need to be more intelligent and restrained about how we use our power. That's Stoicism in the contemporary context. Indeed, Greta Thunberg is the latest in a long line of torchbearers in the race to make humans grow and behave at the same time, all the way back to Socrates.

The conservatives might accuse Greta Thunberg of being too outspoken and progressive. Actually, she is putting forward a view that has been of central importance for us humans throughout history, one that is, in fact, very conservative (with a small c). In order for human civilization to be sustainable, humans need to be less aggressive about how we use the Earth's energy resources. As our powers increase and the Earth becomes a small place compared to our ambitions, we need to take great care of Mother Earth, the secure base for all our explorations.

Humans are making great progress in science, but the fact is that we still don't know a lot about the Earth. Conserving the tropical rainforest is comparatively easy to understand; with its display of biodiversity, including colourful butterflies and birds and shrieking and jumping monkeys, its significance in the Earth's ecosystem is obvious. However, even seemingly barren environments, less attractive in the eyes of humans, harbour hidden treasures in ecosystems that we humans had better respect.

In recent years, deep-sea mining has gained increasing attention due to the potential to access huge amounts of minerals such as manganese, nickel, copper, cobalt and zinc. These minerals are vital to technologies such as solar panels, solar batteries and integrated circuits, products which are considered critical for bringing human civilization to the next stage, while making it more eco-friendly.

Deep-sea mining appears, on the surface, to be quite straightforward and simple. There are golf-ball-shaped objects called polymetallic nodules on the deep ocean floor, and mining consists of picking them up and bringing them to the ocean surface. The depth of the ocean floor (typically thousands of metres beneath its surface) poses some challenges, but with modern robotics technology they are not insurmountable. The problem is, scientists have uncovered a rich ecosystem of life around the deep ocean floor. There are unique species here, not found anywhere else, playing indispensable roles in the maintenance of the environment not only around the ocean floor but also the ocean in general. To complicate matters further, many species actually depend on polymetallic nodules, the very entities that deep-ocean mining is planning to remove, for habitat and nutrition. As a consequence of these discoveries, there is heated debate regarding the planned deep-sea mining at, for example, the Clarion-Clipperton zone in the Pacific Ocean, considered to be one of the largest deposits of polymetallic nodules in the world.

The more we understand the intricate web of the Earth's ecosystem, the less confident we become that our economic activities will not affect them in some unintended and negative ways. Certainly, some might take a cavalier approach to the problem of development and conservation, but there is an increasing number of people who take a more subdued and restrained attitude towards how we humans may make use of the planet Earth.

In 2017, I was attending the TED conference in Vancouver, Canada, and there was a dialogue between Chris Anderson, the TED curator, and Elon Musk. Musk basically stressed the view that in order not to become extinct as a species, we need to spread the human population beyond the Earth, initially to space stations and the moon, and then on to Mars, and eventually to places in the solar system then wider region within the galaxy. Since we don't know what's going to happen to Earth, he argued, we definitely need to have a plan B, or literally a planet B, as part of an overall contingency plan for humanity. Musk has repeatedly expressed his opinion that in addition to spreading the human species as a security measure against possible extinction, the Martian project has the significance of spreading human consciousness across the universe. Musk believes that if human consciousness becomes cosmic in scale, we can perhaps come closer to solving the ultimate questions about life, the universe and everything – rather like the title of one of his favourite Douglas Adams' novels from *The Hitchhiker's Guide to the Galaxy* trilogy (as they are popularly known; or hexalogy, given there are actually six books). According to one analysis, all of Elon Musk's business activities, technological advances and social resources, from Tesla, X (formerly known as Twitter) to SpaceX, are with the final goal of helping humans migrate to Mars and beyond. Musk is certainly a megalomaniac, but one with a rather steadfast track record of achieving what he sets out to do.

I see two attitudes here. On one hand, there is an attitude to treat things, including our planet, as dispensable, an object of trial and error, and if one trial fails, one can move on to the next. On the other hand, there is a call to respect our planet as irreplaceable, the one and only, and cherish it to the end, no matter what happens. Before considering and opting for planet B, we should take better care of planet Earth in the first place.

The truth is, we cannot dispense with planet Earth, no matter how technologically advanced we become. If a human being thinks the Earth is dispensable, it is more likely it's the other way round. The Earth wouldn't care if a human-generated AI race led to technological singularity, posthumanism or transhumanism. (Posthumanism and transhumanism are technological speculations put forward by some technologists about what might come after, or beyond humans, in terms of digital intelligence systems such as AIs and robots.) For the Earth, it would be like a rearrangement of moss on its surface.

The Earth does not care about global warming, either. The most affected will be us humans. After all, the Earth has gone through Snowball Earth periods, when its surface including the tropics was covered with ice and snow, according to the latest scientific theory. After the last Snowball Earth period ended, about 530 million years ago, the Earth went through a period of rapid global warming, and a wide variety of life emerged, in a process called the Cambrian explosion. No matter what folly humans might commit, it doesn't really matter for the Earth. We are not that important.

From a human point of view, needless to say, what we do from here does matter on our humble human scale. That's why we need to listen to Greta Thunberg. That is why we need to be Stoics, and we need to be Earth-bound.

By the way, there are doubts as to whether the plan for

some of us to migrate to Mars would ever really material-
ize, because there is the problem of the brain–gut axis. The
microbiota in our guts are of crucial importance, not only
for the function of the gut itself but also for the brain,
interacting with the gut through the axis. The flora in the
gut, including bacteria, archaea (archaebacteria), fungi and
viruses, come from the Earth's environment. Our whole body
is like a tube, topologically equivalent to an earthworm, and
the internal space of the gut is technically *outside* our body,
continuous with the Earth's environment. If and when some
of us migrate to Mars, the question will be how to bring the
rich and complex microbiota with us. Humans cannot simply
migrate to Mars alone. We need to bring the Earth with us,
encapsulated within our own guts. So there is no planet B,
after all. That should actually be our gut feeling.

Perhaps Elon Musk needs to join Greta Thunberg for an
evening of Japanese *kaiseki* dinner. If one could appreciate the
vast ecosystem of the Earth behind the diverse ingredients at
a typical *kaiseki* sitting, one's technological arrogance might
be slightly curbed.

When I think of the relationship between people and the

Earth, I sometimes think of Ernest Hemingway's masterpiece *The Old Man and the Sea*. In this great novel, the old man is coming face to face with Mother Earth, single-handedly, without the help of any technologies. In the way that the old man uses his energy, resources, attention and actions to align with the Earth's environment, he is a true Stoic. He would not even dream of planet B. The Earth is his whole universe. He is an Earth-bound Stoic, as I hope we all can be.

CHAPTER 14

Stoicism and the universe

In 1999, American social psychologists Justin Kruger and David Dunning jointly published a paper titled 'Unskilled and Unaware of It: How Difficulties in Recognizing One's Own Incompetence Lead to Inflated Self-Assessments', in which they described the finding that the less skilled are overconfident and tend to overestimate their performances, while the more skilled are humble and tend to underestimate theirs. Their finding, which came to be known as the Dunning-Kruger effect, became widely known among the general public, and has been used to account for the puzzlingly overconfident behaviours of people from politicians to internet trolls. The Stoic, needless to say, strives to be free from the Dunning-Kruger effect.

Socrates, the father of Stoicism, was always stressing that he knew nothing, which attitude came to be known as Socratic ignorance. Being intelligent is an open-ended endeavour, and the more you know, the less confident about the world you become. Knowledge is like a handle on the unknown, and as your knowledge becomes deep, so you become more aware of your own ignorance. Issac Newton was arguably one of the most intelligent people in the history of humankind, and yet this very humble reflection on what he has achieved tells us about the humility that necessarily accompanies a great intellect:

> I do not know what I may appear to the world, but to myself I seem to have been only like a boy playing on the sea-shore, and diverting myself in now and then finding a smoother pebble or a prettier shell than ordinary, whilst the great ocean of truth lay all undiscovered before me.

In the context of the make-up of human intelligence, we talk about Newtonian uncertainty: the more you know, the more uncertain the world becomes. When Newton mentioned the 'great ocean of truth ... undiscovered', he presumably had a premonition of what could come long after his time on this Earth is over, with associated domains of uncertainty. Within that uncertainty lay the theory of relativity that Albert Einstein developed, which superseded the Newtonian concept of space-time. And Einstein, in turn, had a similar premonition of the unknown. He once remarked:

The most beautiful thing we can experience is the mysterious. It is the source of all true art and science. He to whom the emotion is a stranger, who can no longer pause to wonder and stand wrapped in awe, is as good as dead – his eyes are closed.

Einstein's 'the mysterious' corresponds to Newton's 'great ocean of truth ... undiscovered'. And now, more than 100 years after Einstein's 1915 publication of the general theory of relativity, which accounted for the space-time structure of the universe, physicists and cosmologists are seriously discussing the implications of dark matter and dark energy, unexpected and mysterious aspects of the universe which Einstein actually introduced. Einstein suggested the idea of a cosmological constant in 1917 in order to account for the properties of the observed universe but later called it the 'biggest blunder' in his life. Now, dark energy, which is basically the energy of the vacuum, is regarded as a full-forced revival of Einstein's cosmological constant. Indeed, Einstein's cosmological constant is mathematically equivalent to contemporary ideas about dark matter and dark energy. The problem is, nobody understands the exact nature of this mysterious property of the space-time – yet. It is great that humans have made huge progress in the understanding of the universe, yet at the same time, we are aware, more than ever in history, of our utter ignorance about the world we inhabit.

In discussing the merits of intelligent humility, it is perhaps fitting to refer to people who have tackled the problems of the universe, like Newton and Einstein, as nothing makes us more humble than to think about our place in the universe. Marcus Aurelius, in *Meditations*, repeatedly writes about the cosmic void surrounding our lives. We humans occasionally might have the hubris to believe that we are the masters of everything, but in reality we are just an insignificant part of the whole cosmos. We are not at the centre of the universe. Indeed, we are just a grain of sand in the great ocean of existence.

The mediocrity principle, originally attributed to German astrophysicist Sebastian Rudolf Karl von Hoerner, states that there should be nothing special about humans. In 1961, von Hoerner observed that 'Anything seemingly unique and peculiar to us is actually one out of many and is probably average'. There is a statistical reasoning behind von Hoerner's humble assessment of humanity. If we take a random sample from the universe, statistically, it is likely to be average. We happen to live in this particular solar system, but its evolution and make-up are likely to be quite mediocre among the many similar systems in the universe. Likewise, the evolution of life leading to humanity would have been quite average. The conclusion is that there is probably nothing uniquely special about humans, although we tend to assume there is.

The mediocrity principle gives us the statistical justification for being humble. It is a statistical version of Stoicism, if you like.

It can, perhaps, also make us feel helpless.

The vast extent of the universe is intimidating to contemplate. Seneca lamented the shortness of time. When people around us say this, it is usually intended to mean that we waste too much time doing meaningless things, and perhaps we really do. But Seneca meant it in more absolute ways. And when we consider the nature of time as revealed by science today on the cosmic scale, his lamentation seems justified. The universe is about 13.8 billion years old, whereas our personal time on this Earth is likely to be about 100 years at most. As Stoics, we cannot help noticing that the picture science draws of the universe today is rather unnerving.

Modern physics suggests that our existence is literally a miracle balanced on a very fragile condition. The multiverse theory, a controversial and yet powerful model of the world as we know it, states that our particular universe is just one of a multitude of possible worlds that could, and perhaps actually do, exist. We are all here because the physical parameters such as the gravitational constant, electron mass and electrical charge on Earth are fine-tuned just so. If the relevant parameters were altered even slightly, the universe would be differently formed, with no stars like the sun to give out energy or planets like the Earth to start life on. The universe would be just a barren and uninteresting extension of space. Life as we know it would not be able to exist at all. The gist of the multiverse theory is that there is no particular reason why the physical parameters of Earth are fine-tuned in favour of life on Earth, the evolution of which would lead to humanity. The parameters and the universe could have been configured in any number of ways, and there are other universes with different parameters. We just happen to be living in one of them, which just happens to be favorable to our existence.

Not only that, we happen to live in a miraculously timed moment of this particular universe. Ever since the Big Bang about 13.8 billion years ago, the universe has been expanding. Recent evidence suggests that the expansion is actually accelerating, due to the mysterious existence of the aforementioned dark energy and dark matter. At present, we have no definite theoretical account of why dark energy and matter exist, but we do need to assume their existence in order to account for the formation and behaviours of stellar bodies, including the multitude of galaxies in the universe. In any case, if we believe our current understanding of the universe, it is likely to keep expanding, in an accelerated manner, until, billions of years from now, a mere fifty times its existing age of 13.8 billion years by some estimates, there will only be few remaining chunks of matter, with vast distances in between, and the whole universe would be just a desert of nothingness, for ever and ever.

There is something cruel and absurd about the picture that modern physics and cosmology paint for the future of our universe. It is cruel, because all life, including human life, is bound to be crushed or evaporate. It is absurd, because the universe doesn't care about these things. The universe does not care about the fact that we are here, discussing Stoicism together, at this difficult juncture of human history. Yet there is also something paradoxically soothing about the fact that, no matter how hard we try, no matter what efforts we might make, nothingness is the basic fabric of reality for this universe, and all humanity. Years from now, nobody, or nothing in the universe will remember us, just as we don't remember the multitude of life that came before us.

This kind of thinking is the territory of the seventeenth-century French mathematician and philosopher Blaise Pascal. Pascal, who was most definitely a Stoic, suggested in his writings that we are just a reed, exposed to the brutal forces of the universe. Here are his famous words:

The human being is only a reed, the most feeble in nature; but this is a thinking reed. It isn't necessary for the entire universe to arm itself in order to crush him; a whiff of vapor, a taste of water, suffices to kill him. But when the universe crushes him, the human being becomes still more noble than that which kills him, because he knows that he is dying, and the advantage that the universe has over him. The universe, it does not have a clue.

Here, the great thinker has captured the essential condition of our existence in this universe. We are at the mercy of the brutal forces of nature, and our consciousness is like a tiny *medaka* fish in a small pond, formed by a spell of rainfall in the evening of an otherwise scorching hot land.

Our habitable domain of space-time is very limited and will soon dry up. However, as long as the tiny water pool lasts, the *medaka* fish will do its best to live, to feed and to propagate. Such is exactly the situation we find ourselves in, and our world view needs to be aligned with this reality. That is actually central to the spirit of Stoicism.

But wait. There is a silver lining in this dark cloud of cosmic existential nihilism. Although this interpretation of the universe is undoubtedly harsh, it might paradoxically lead to an optimistic world view, if we embrace it from a Stoic perspective. For the darker the picture of the whole universe is, the brighter, more precious and more valuable our own lives appear to be. As we embrace our brief, precarious existence in the vast extension of space-time we call the universe, the feeling of living in the here and now is not so bad.

It is a miracle. A joke. Absurd.

This is indeed the ultra-cosmic world view of absurdity.

I once had the wonderful experience of having a chat with Matt Lucas and David Walliams when they made a visit to Tokyo. The comics were at the height of their fame as creators and stars of *Little Britain*. There were many things about them that deeply impressed me. One of the defining moments in our meeting was when Matt Lucas said his comedy originated as a defence mechanism. At school, he was often laughed at. Rather than allowing himself to become the victim of the malicious laughter, Lucas resorted to a more creative solution. He started to *make* people laugh.

Quite possibly, the universe does not care about humanity enough to even laugh at us. But perhaps we might use laughter as our cosmic defence mechanism.

Douglas Adams' *The Hitchhiker's Guide to the Galaxy* is one of the best comic defences against the absurdity of the universe. It has a famous storyline in which humanity asks a supercomputer the answer to the 'Ultimate Question of Life, the Universe, and Everything'. After 7.5 million years of calculation, humans gather around the computer to finally know the answer. First the computer answers '42'. Then, seeing that humans are not entirely impressed or convinced by its answer, the computer suggests they calculate the 'Ultimate Question of Life, the Universe, and Everything' themselves. So, the Earth is set up as a supercomputer to do this, but unfortunately, just five minutes before the calculation is completed, the Earth is destroyed to make way for a new hyperspace bypass.

Cosmic laughter as depicted in *The Hitchhiker's Guide to the Galaxy* is a wonderful reaction to the fundamentally absurd situation we find ourselves in in this universe. When you think about the universe as a whole, we humans quite literally don't matter. I don't matter, you don't matter, she doesn't matter, he doesn't matter and they don't matter. Nothing matters. This calls for a comic spirit, a bit of laughter – indeed, a lot of laughter. The more profound our despair becomes, in the face of the absurdity of the universe, the more explosive the expression of comic spirit will need to be in reaction. Socrates had a great sense of humour. A Stoic must laugh.

CHAPTER 15

Stoicism and accepting death

In Japan, the samurai class had the philosophy that a samurai must accept his own death when honour required it. *Hagakure*, an eighteenth-century book describing *bushidō*, the ethical code of the samurai, described it as a way of dying and declared that 'the way of the warrior is the way to die'. Needless to say, a samurai's death was not meant as a random, insignificant act. *Bushidō* was about recognizing that precise moment of self-obliteration, most typically during the course of a battle with an enemy, but sometimes through the act of *seppuku*, an honourable way of taking one's own life. When that time came, it was considered the right thing to do, for a samurai, to be prepared to let go of his own life. In that sense, it was an ultimate way to be aligned with something bigger than oneself – a true spirit of Stoicism.

The samurai approach to one's own death might not immediately seem appropriate in today's world. In the past, there have been misrepresentations of the stated codes of actions. The high-profile death of Yukio Mishima by *seppuku* in 1970 gave a bitter aftertaste to the literary career of this novelist of brilliant talents. Yet, although the samurai's way of facing death is open to many questions and concerns today, it remains one of the most impressive examples of a Stoic's attitude towards death, in a world where eventual death is inevitable for all living beings and there are causes larger than one's life.

The acceptance of one's death might be considered one of the hallmarks of the Stoic attitude. In ancient Greece, Socrates accepted his own death ordered by the state with calm. Likewise, Seneca accepted *his* death ordered by the Roman Emperor Nero. And even when the cause of death is natural, a Stoic will accept it in a spirit of resignation. Indeed, as a Stoic, it is one of the ultimate signs of maturity to accept the natural course of one's life and not fight against it.

Yet the Promethean attitude of some scientists and technologists today appears to be quite the opposite, in that they seek to overcome the mortality of human life. It seems that many actually do pursue the illusory goal of the eternal life. The illusion is that strong.

However, given that the universe is expanding with acceleration, and will ultimately become a vast void with nothing interesting going on (see Chapter 14), seeking eternal life does not make sense.

Others might say that it is overkill to rule out the possibility of eternal life from the point of view of the ultimate fate of the universe. While I certainly understand that objection, Stoicism is about aligning one's life with the ultimate truth of the universe. From the Stoic point of view, seeking eternal life can only serve as another proxy goal. Indeed, if Socrates was alive today, he might interrogate someone who pursues this using the Socratic method:

'What do you mean you want eternal life?'
'What does it mean if everyone else dies and you are
    the only one alive?

215

'Do you know the ultimate fate of the universe?

'Do you mean that you want to outlive the universe?

'Is it OK that you are going to live forever, but you
did not exist before you were born?'

I have encountered only one person who answered the question about outliving the universe in the affirmative. I was teaching at the Tokyo University of the Arts for a while, and at one time the Japanese conceptual artist Shusaku Arakawa came to give a lecture. To a classroom of enchanted students, Arakawa started to talk passionately about art. He was seeking eternal life through art, he declared. He talked with such force that bits of his saliva were sprinkled all around. 'There are billions of life forms in my saliva,' Arakawa said. 'Like those tiny creatures, I am never going to die. Even when the universe ends, I am going to live! Oh, yes, I am going to outlive the universe, through my art form!' A few years after this pledge for eternal life in a packed lecture room at the Tokyo University of the Arts, Arakawa passed away. When I heard the news, strangely, I felt no sense of contradiction. Maybe

Arakawa is living, in some strange way, and he *will* outlive the universe somehow.

Some seek to achieve eternal life through science and technology. Research is being conducted into mind uploading, in which researchers propose to scan the human brain to obtain information about the synaptic connections between neurons and then upload the data to a digital computer. It is proposed that, by conducting a whole-brain emulation, in which the dynamics of neural activities are reproduced and simulated, a digital copy of the brain can be created. Some claim that this would give rise to a digital consciousness, which, unlike the real brain, could be copied and propagated, eventually for eternity.

One of the practical problems with mind uploading is that it is not easy to obtain data about the synaptic connections of the whole brain. In particular, it is difficult to do it with a living, functioning brain. Some researchers claim that they could, in principle, map the neural network architecture to digital data by scanning using microscopy and reconstructing techniques, but that would have to be conducted post-mortem.

In 2018, a start-up called *Nectome* offered to scan people's brains and digitally upload the data with one caveat – it was '100 per cent fatal'. After heavy criticism from the neuro-science community, MIT media lab severed connections with the start-up.

The fact is, the claims of mind uploading remain highly speculative, and the majority of researchers studying the human brain agree that the very idea of it, i.e. transferring data from the brain to create a digital consciousness, is likely to remain a scientific pipe dream. For one thing, it is not clear what is meant by obtaining and uploading data. What data? You may take the view that obtaining the synaptic weights between neurons and then running a simulation of how the neural network dynamics would evolve would be necessary and sufficient. In this so-called connectionist approach, neurons interacting with synapses are assumed to be the equivalent of cognition and consciousness, but that is an incomplete description of what actually goes on in the brain. There are many other parameters possibly rel-evant to the real brain in generating consciousness. Within one single neuron, there are multitudes of processes going on – for example, water molecules moving around, proteins colliding into each other, electromagnetic fields permeating the whole space and genes being transcribed and modified. Out of this cacophony of activity, there is no telling which particular subsets of parameters are relevant for reproducing consciousness. Maybe we need all of them, rather than simulating some of them.

Even if one were able to successfully capture all the relevant information in a brain at a particular time (the achievability of which is doubtful), there is the question of how to simulate temporal evolution from there. Just a very small difference in the initial condition, as time passes, could lead to a very large difference in the state of the system – another instance of the butterfly effect. In reality, any simulation is only an approximation. When the simulation concerns the weather, then conducting an approximation makes practical sense, as we all know from weather forecasts. In this instance, a rough idea of what the weather will be like tomorrow is better than no idea. It does not make sense, however, to say that we are going to approximate the consciousness of a person. If the simulated state of consciousness differs from the actual conscious mind, what does it even mean? Which is the real consciousness – the actual person or the simulated one?

Finally, there is the question of the simulated brain's interactions with the outside world. Say you could successfully retrieve all information about a brain, and you could successfully run a more or less accurate simulation of it (which is always an approximation), then what would happen to the outside world with which the brain interacts? When it comes to brain function, literally, no man is an island, entire of itself. The brain is an open system, and needs to interact with the world to function properly. Does mind uploading mean that we are also going to simulate the world, too? Even if we simulated only the local environment, then the possible range of interaction would expand with the passage of time; specifically, the possible range of influence would spread with the speed of light. In principle, if you want to simulate ten years of environmental influences on a particular brain, you would have to simulate a world with a radius of ten light years. Is it even possible, or, for that matter, worthwhile to do so? The more you think about the premises behind mind uploading, the less it makes sense. It might be arguably be one of the most ridiculous ideas in human history.

The ups and downs about mind uploading, including the MIT start-up fiasco, seem to me to reflect a larger disease of our time. Too many people equate simulation with reality. Stoicism, as we know, is about aligning with the true nature of the universe. A Stoic takes reality seriously; simulation, on the other hand, has nothing to do with it per se. It is an art of make believe.

The problem is not with the concept of simulation itself. Simulating something so that we can better predict the outcome has tremendous practical significance. For example, simulating trends of global warming due to the presence of carbon dioxide provides crucial information for our future. From traffic control to global economy, modern human life cannot function without large-scale simulations, and kudos should be given to the science of simulation in general.

Simulations, however, are not real things. Simulations are fakes, with practical uses for prediction. It is one of the worst illusions of the human mind to take a fake for the real thing, especially as regards the most essential element of our existence: consciousness.

At the most absurd end of this craze for simulation, there is this idea that the whole world, the whole universe we live in, is a simulation. Some argue, notably the Swedish philosopher Nick Bostrom, that it is more likely than not that we live in a simulation. This 'simulation hypothesis' represents one of the most vulnerable and fragile intellectual premises of our time. It shows how far some of us have deviated from the Stoic way, with the kind of healthy scepticism exhibited by Socrates.

The fallacy of the simulation hypothesis resides in the very foundation of what a simulation actually means. There are inherent assumptions, shared by people who argue for mind uploading and simulation hypothesis, about what information is, what a representation of information entails and what it means to physically implement that representation. For example, simulating global weather on a digital computer just means that you have a representation of it on silicon chips, the dynamics of which can be interpreted to make predictions about the weather. It does not mean anything more than that. To say that there is anything you would be able to call real weather emerging from that simulation on silicon chips is a cognitive failure too naive to be taken seriously by a Stoic. Socrates would have found it a great ironic joke.

Finally, some of those who take a naive view about simulation are discussing plans to preserve a deceased person digitally forever, so that the bereaved friends and families can keep interacting with them. If you have followed the arguments in this book, you would immediately see the flaws in such a logic (I hope). It is a sadly shallow scheme, and a sacrilege of life.

I do understand the motives behind such attempts. We all miss our loved ones when they pass away. While it is quite understandable that some of us desire to keep interacting with them post-mortem, it would be difficult to envisage ways to reproduce and preserve, in any meaningful sense, the vivid personal impressions, the idiosyncratic ways and ever-changing interactions with a live person. The idea of digital eternal life might be one of the most futile illusions of our time, most sadly so, when it is purportedly applied to the preservation of the life of a deceased person.

Whether you are an emperor, a slave or an ordinary citizen, a scientist, a technologist or a samurai, death is inevitable. If we see these things clearly, we might be able to live a Stoic life. On the other hand, if we let the fear of death blur our minds, it might lead to the kind of illusions I have discussed in this chapter. If we believe in these delusions, we might have a momentary feeling of satisfaction. However, sooner or later, the false sense of security will evaporate, like a thin layer of water under the scorching sun of reality.

From the Stoic point of view, aligning with reality is the only way to live.

Life is not a simulation.

The universe is not a simulation.

We do not live in a simulation.

Period.

CHAPTER 16

The best of all possible worlds

Stoicism is a way to live in alignment with reality. There's no escaping it. However, that is not to say that dreams and fantasies do not have a place in human existence. Adults may laugh at wishful thinking, but there is something genuinely human about imagining things outside of the reality of this world.

When I was just out of college, I was returning from a trip to one of the local cities in Japan one morning. Upon arriving at Tokyo's Haneda Airport, I went into a curry restaurant to have breakfast. It was near the holiday season in December, and the Christmas decorations and lights were up. In Japan, where people take more or less relaxed and open attitudes towards cultural elements from abroad, Christmas is celebrated big time, although only about one per cent of Japanese identify themselves as Christians in the traditional sense.

There was a family near my table, including a girl of about five years old and her younger sister, aged about three. As I ate my curry, I overheard their conversation.

'What do you think Mr Santa Claus is like?' asked the five-year-old of her younger sister. Without waiting for an answer (perhaps she never expected one), she went on, 'I think that Santa looks like . . .'

I was struck on the spot – so moved I couldn't pay close attention to their conversation any more. My mind was full of thoughts.

There is something genuinely sincere about children fantasizing about imaginary characters like Santa Claus. There are popular descriptions of Father Christmas, with a fat belly, white beard, red costume and jolly laugh. However, when children imagine Santa Claus, they seem to go beyond the conventional image. There is something wildly free in the children's fantasies, and that perhaps has a lot to do with the origin of creativity. Children project their innermost desires on to the character of Santa Claus.

As we have discussed, children need a secure base for their development. Obviously, it would be great for every child to start from one, raised by loving caretakers, most typically their parents, who would, among other things, give them a present at Christmas. However, not every child is fortunate enough to have loving caretakers. Some might have nobody around to love them or give them a present on Christmas morning. The illusion of Santa Claus would be of great help for such children. Needless to say, there are limits to what imagination alone can do, but children thrive on their imaginations, as anyone who has been a child (by which I mean all of us) will testify. In the real world, they might not have a secure base, but the imaginary character of Santa Claus would provide for them. And even for a child who does have loving parents, imagining Santa Claus could make their secure base stronger, and provide for a rainy day.

As we grow up, at some stage we become disenchanted, at least as far as Santa Claus goes. In other aspects, adults might continue to be illusioned, sometimes in quite sophisticated grown-up ways, but ceasing to believe in Santa Claus is usually considered to be a sign of maturity and the end of a healthy childhood, at least in Western cultures. So, it was particularly fascinating for me to learn how Japanese theatre and film director and actor Yukio Ninagawa went a long way towards keeping the fantasy of Santa Claus alive for his daughter Mika Ninagawa, a photographer and director widely known in her own right. I once had a chat with Mika for a TV programme. When we were discussing her father, she told me how each year, he would create a different script and setting for Santa, presented with various directions for Mika to follow, so that there would be always some surprises beyond her expectations. Incredibly, Ninagawa successfully made his daughter Mika believe in Santa Claus well into her teens. It is a great story of fatherly love mingled with the genius of a world-class theatre director.

But how does this fit with the Stoic approach to life, which is proudly based on facts and realities? Stoic thinkers, including Socrates, Epictetus, Seneca and Marcus Aurelius, repeatedly remarked that we need to accept the world as it is. We need to acknowledge people around us as they are. We need to accept the fact that nobody is perfect, including our-selves. Even when we learn that Santa Claus does not exist, we carry on, immersing ourselves in the practical world, unless we are the great theatre director Yukio Ninagawa, in which case we go to extraordinary efforts to make him a reality for a beloved daughter. Could it be that fantasies such as Santa Claus resonate deeply within us because they make our reality a little more bearable?

Karen Carpenter (of the Carpenters fame) sang, 'I ask perfection of a quite imperfect world'. Who doesn't do this? The sense that we know what a perfect world is, and that *this* is actually an imperfect world, is one of the strongest intuitions that we have from childhood. Many cultures have a conception of a perfect world. In the Christian tradition there is the Garden of Eden from which Adam and Eve were expelled. In the Chinese tradition there is the utopia of the Peach Blossom Spring, an idyllic paradise where people live in complete harmony. China even has a specific idealized period in its history ruled by legendary rulers Yao, Shun and Yu. It is only human to seek an idealized state of affairs in the real world. However, as lessons in history tell us, seeking earthly utopia typically ends in tears. That Santa Claus exists would be perfection, but the fact that he does not is the unavoidable imperfect reality.

As I have discussed in Chapters 4 and 5, accepting our limitations and those of others is a powerful function of the prefrontal cortex of the brain. Our neural circuits, including the amygdala, put various negative feelings into an appropriate context as a way of coming to terms with our emotions. By the process of reappraisal, we may become reconciled with people and things that we can otherwise find difficult to take in as they are. This is also one of the central tenets of Stoicism.

But in addition to this coming to terms with emotions, we may need to perform a cognitive reappraisal of the world. In fact, if we think our imperfect reality through in a logically coherent manner, as any Stoic should do, the conclusion turns out to be something rather counterintuitive and surprising. Far from seeing the flaws and limitations in our situation, we might find that we are actually living in the best of all possible worlds. This might sound like a strange idea at first, but you will begin to see the profound Stoic wisdom and vision behind it once you start to think about it. The Stoic belief is that no matter which country you are born in or what kind of conditions you find yourself living in, you live in the best of all possible worlds.

This idea – a viewpoint sometimes called philosophical optimism – was first framed by Gottfried Wilhelm Leibniz (1646–1716). Leibniz was a man of many talents, who engaged himself in mathematics, science and philosophy and was also active in diplomacy. Most notably, he invented differential and integral calculus, independently of Isaac Newton, at approximately the same time. (There has been debate, initiated by Newton himself, on whether Leibniz took ideas from him, but modern scholarship generally agrees that Leibniz's calculus was an independent invention in its own right.)

Even at the time, philosophical optimism had its critics, particularly the writer Voltaire, whose world view had been deeply shaken by the great Lisbon earthquake and tsunami that struck Portugal in 1755, killing about 60,000 people in Lisbon alone. For Voltaire, this shuddering experience turned into a motive for criticizing Leibniz. He used his satirical novel *Candide*, in which the comical figure of Professor

Pangloss advocates the optimistic view that this is the best of all possible worlds, to mock Leibniz's philosophy. Needless to say, *Candide* ends with the complete collapse of Pangloss's ideology.

As someone who lives in Japan, a country where devastating earthquakes and tsunamis happen, I can certainly sympathize with Voltaire. How can one say that a world in which terrible natural disasters take place, that claim the lives of tens of thousands of innocent people, is the best of all possible worlds?

If you face reality, you know that in addition to natural calamities, this world is full of social problems and injustices. Can you really say, 'Don't worry, you are living in the best of all possible worlds' to a person suffering from the oppression of an unfair political system, or someone who is the victim of discrimination? We always need to strive for the improvement of human conditions.

But Leibniz's philosophical optimism (and here you will instantly see how it relates to Stoicism) is concerned with the logical and systemic connections of things. We may say that certain things are bad for humanity, and wish that the world could be a better place without them – from the vision of the Garden of Eden to the idealized period in Chinese history of the legendary rulers Yao, Shun and Yu, we have always envisioned a world where there is no evil or misfortune – but if we see how things are causally connected to each other, we cannot simply advocate for the removal of a subset of the system, even if it is manifestly evil. The interdependency of good and bad is too intricate.

Take cancer. According to the World Health Organization, cancer is the second-leading cause of death in the world, accounting for about one in six deaths. It is natural for humans to wish that there would be a world without cancer. As the British comedian Stephen Fry once asked, how can there be a God when there are children suffering from cancer? He was arguing for atheism based on the perceived imperfections of the world, which could not be the workings of a well-intending God. Surely, as Fry says, a world with cancer cannot be the best of all possible worlds.

However, things look a little more complicated when we ponder the causal connections. The aspects of cellular physiology and the molecular dynamics that lead to cancer are the same set of dynamics that supports our normal bodily functions. Indeed, one may even say that without the cellular physiology that creates the potential for cancer, we could not live at all in the first place. That's why it is so difficult to overcome cancer, as its very mechanisms are deeply embedded in cellular functions.

The same goes for earthquakes. As I mentioned, coming from Japan, where earthquakes and tsunamis have repeatedly caused major devastation, I know only too well the damage that could be inflicted. However, we cannot simply say that we would be better off without earthquakes. The geophysical processes that lead to earthquakes from time to time are causally coupled with those that lead to the formation and shift of continents. Without earthquakes, we would not have land masses to live on in the first place. As a side effect, we also have hot springs, enjoyed as *onsen* in Japanese culture and increasingly also popular among visitors from abroad and, occasionally, enjoyed by the snow monkeys.

Philosophical optimism, as suggested by Leibniz, counsels accepting things such as earthquakes and cancer as integral parts of the world we live in. As a first reaction to negative events in life, it is natural to wish that they did not occur. However, if we observe the world as it is, we must come to the conclusion that things, including negative occurrences, are interwoven into its fabric. We simply cannot cherry-pick the good bits from the world, because it is an organic whole. Thus, the adjective 'best' in the phrase 'best of all possible worlds' does not necessarily mean it is 'best' according to the value system of human well-being. It is 'best' in the sense that everything is connected, and working in such subtle and coordinated ways, that there is a balance overall which cannot be separated so easily.

The same could be said for social issues. When we perceive unfairness and injustice in society, we are naturally disappointed and would love to see the issues improved. However, the solution might not lie in the simple removal of the perceived evils. Things might be interconnected in so many surprising ways that, if we want social reform, we need to be mindful of the intricate web of causal connections. To say that the status quo is the best of all possible worlds – to accept the interconnected reality, both good and bad – is the best position from which to make a long, patient and careful ascent, because acceptance of reality is the best basis for change, rather than wishing the world was different.

It is important to stress that I am not advocating a defeatist attitude here. We do need to keep making efforts towards a better future. There is no doubt that it would be great to have more democracy, for example, so that people could live more freely, liberated from oppression, and respect each other's individuality and uniqueness.

The point is to see how things are connected clearly; in the Stoic sense, to see how they align. If we understand the connections between things, then we realize that the world cannot be understood as a simple black and white dichotomy. The reality is fifty or more shades of grey, or even more nuanced spectrum of things.

Let's say a country is divided into two, with one half a democracy and the other an authoritarian regime; you would probably want to live in the former. Such differences in government might lead to gaps in economic growth. When seen from a satellite at night, the democratic half might be lit up, while the other remains in darkness, bearing witness to its sluggish economy. Such a contrast would typically suggest that the democratic political system is superior. However, there might be upsides to the darker half, such as less depleted natural habitat, and less impact on global climate. Crucially, if you happened to live in the undemocratic part of the country, there is nothing for it but for you to do your best in that given situation, in the spirit of *ganbaru*. Of course, eventually, you may take extraordinary actions, such as trying to escape the country, or working to bring about social reform. As many anecdotes suggest, such measures can be very difficult and dangerous and are not necessarily recommended for any random person.

No matter what kind of situation you might find yourself in, you need to make the best of it somehow, because that's all you have got, for the time being. In this respect, Leibniz's best-of-all-possible-worlds argument is an understanding that everything is aligned, but also a call for a proactive, resilient spirit. That's why it belongs to this book on Stoicism. It also has an important link to Claude Lévi-Strauss's *bricolage*, or its Japanese equivalent *nora*.

A corollary of the arguments that I have put forward in this chapter would be that you are the best of all possible persons, and that you are living the best of all possible lives. As we have seen, this is not an emotional lullaby to soothe the soul, but the result of a rigorous, thorough and logical analysis of how things are interconnected, and how any unique set of traits, whether it is of an individual human being or a nation, has its merits and shortcomings.

You are the best of all possible persons, living the best of all possible lives, in the best of all possible worlds.

After reading this chapter, I hope that the statement above does not sound so fantastic or extraordinary. You may well be disappointed if you ask perfection of a quite imperfect world, but if you start your day in a spirit of philosophical optimism with the perception that yours is the best of all possible worlds, you can exhibit the *ganbaru* spirit like a good Stoic.

CHAPTER 17

Facing the infinite

Our lives in this world are limited. And yet, we can perceive and appreciate unlimited things. In a sense, Stoicism is about us humans, the finite, aligning with the universe, the infinite. For most of us, infinity is just a distant concept. As children, we love asking about infinity, giving adults a hard time by quizzing them about the beginning and the end of time, and the outside of the universe, but as we grow up, we become practical and forget to ask those infinity questions. There is one profession, however, whose job description includes facing the infinite. For mathematicians, facing infinity is all in a day's work and they share a peculiarly keen sense of the infinite.

Mathematicians probably cannot be said to be typical of humanity, but the results of their confrontations with infinity are all around us. The Global Positioning System, or GPS for short, is an indispensable tool that everybody now uses on their smartphones all the time. But without considering time dilations, as described by the mathematics of the general theory of relativity developed by Einstein, when analyzing the signals received from the satellites, the positioning by GPS cannot be accurate. The RSA (Rivest–Shamir–Adleman) cryptosystem, which is widely used in secure data communications today, was designed by three computer science/mathematics experts, Ron Rivest, Adi Shamir and Leonard Adleman, based on the mathematics of prime factors. Penrose tiling, a mathematical construct of tiles proposed by British mathematician and Nobel laureate Roger Penrose, which covers an infinite plane in an aperiodic manner and has a five-fold rotational symmetry, appears in nature as quasicrystals.

Mathematicians mentally live in a world distant from the everyday life of typical humans and that seems to make some of them strangely optimistic. Teiji Takagi was a prominent Japanese mathematician who studied with the German mathematician David Hilbert, sometimes referred to as 'the father of modern mathematics'. In an essay, Takagi recollected a conversation with Hilbert on a visit to the latter's home in Göttingen in 1900, in which Hilbert repeatedly told Takagi that 'milliards' (an old expression for billions) of years are available for human progress, so we would hopefully make great advancements. It says something about a mathematician's sense of infinity that Hilbert had the audacity to hope that great changes were going to come to humanity someday 'soon' (from a mathematician's perspective).

It is liberating and uplifting to think about mathematics, mathematicians and their rather peculiar ways of dealing with the world. If the mission of a Stoic is to perceive the nature of existence as it actually is, and to embrace the human condition to the full, mathematical reasoning is obviously part of the equation.

Without addressing the problems of the infinite, we cannot deal with the core essence of the restlessness of reason (which we will discuss in detail in the next chapter) that we grapple with in our souls. At a time when we are learning about the sheer absurdity of the vast universe as a scientific fact, we do need to learn how to face infinity, as a matter of existential urgency.

If you face the reality of this world in a sincere way, then you will realize that we humans are actually surrounded by infinities. Aristotle discussed two kinds of infinity. One is actual infinity, and the other is potential infinity. Actual infinity is impossible for humans to handle, because our capacities are limited by finite resources. The human mind can think about actual infinity, but it can never be embodied. We are, however, able to handle potential infinity through our actions in daily life. Indeed, from a Stoic position, dealing with potential infinity is a way of living, both in the philosophical and practical sense, in which our lives are aligned with the principles of space and time.

Potential infinity is accessible through focusing on the next step. In the process of mathematical induction, if a proposition holds for n, and if it can be shown to hold for $n+1$, then we can prove that it will hold for an infinite number of cases. This is the way mathematics deals with actual infinity – by means of potential infinity. The assurance of the next step eventually leads to a truthful statement for infinite numbers.

Thus, we may access actual infinity through potential infinity. Indeed, in the human mind, potential infinity functions as the handle on actual infinity.

In a very practical sense, this means you may access infinity in life, as long as you have a clear idea about what your next step will be. In that context, it is crucially important to make sure that you always have something to do next at any moment. When you wake up in the morning, if you know what to do first, and then do the next thing after that, followed by something else and so on, until you rest at night, then you are in possession of potential infinity. This is a very Stoic way to live.

Potential infinity is in how we choose what to do next. At the start of this book, I discussed the choice overload we typically face today. But as long as we can choose our next action appropriately, we can hope to access potential infinity, even in a situation affected by choice overload.

Stoicism is when your next action makes sense. As long as your actions are aligned with your life's purposes, and do not affect the environment in any adversarial ways, it is going to be stoically all right.

In Chapter 3, you may remember I discussed next token prediction, which basically predicts, given a series of word inputs, what word sequences would come next. Next token prediction is behind the incredible abilities exhibited by generative AIs, in particular Large Language Models (LLMs) such as ChatGPT. In a similar vein, we may consider next action prediction as the basis of a Stoic way of life, in which we apply potential infinity in our lives. Given the series of previous actions, and the context of the particular situation, what series of actions is likely to follow? If, every day of our lives, we apply next action prediction and execute the predicted action, then we will achieve the state of the flow described by Mihaly Csikszentmihalyi, as well as a constant connection to potential infinity.

As we advance in the history of humanity, we may keep up infinite progress, literally. That might sound like a grandiose prediction to those worried about possible human extinction due to global warming, nuclear war and artificial intelligence, but a Stoic (and a mathematician) would remain optimistic, even in difficult situations.

If you are not a mathematician (which is the case for most

of us) and mathematics is not your cup of tea, don't worry. The beauty of mathematics is that it applies to people who don't care about it, too. As you go about your life, doing your job, having your cup of coffee, taking a walk, listening to music, meeting people, looking up at the sky, the potential infinity discussed in this chapter is always with you. You don't even have to think about it. It is just there, like a cat coming around the next corner of the street.

In order to face the infinite, choosing your next action is crucial. Take the next step. That would constitute your life's potential infinity.

CHAPTER 18

All roads lead to Socrates

As you may recall, although the Stoic school as we know it started from Zeno of Citium, the movement is not known by the founder's name, but rather derived from the *stoa*, or painted porch, where Zeno taught his ideas in ancient Athens. Some say that this was to avoid a cult of personality – a mindset of staying away from a potential danger that we could learn from today.

If you look back on the history of the world, this negation of the cult of personality appears to be an exception to the rule. No matter where you look throughout history, we have worshipped individuals, with few qualms expressed about that trend.

In today's zeitgeist, in which there is a craze for gathering followers, likes, views, etc. on social media, the cult of personality is the norm rather than the outlier. In the attention economy, likes and views turn into real money, and it truly does mean business. It is no wonder that some people are obsessed with these social media metrics, especially if they crave fame and money.

Any serious attempt to understand and make one's own Stoicism today should therefore involve keeping a distance from the attention economy. Sure, it might be nice to draw some attention to your work, if it is the result of something genuine and close to your heart – the fruit of your *ikigai*. But to seek attention for the sake of it, and forget what it was all about in the first place, is futile. (One may remember Goodhart's Law here, discussed in Chapter 11, which states that when a measure becomes a target, it ceases to be a good measure. This is a great caution for anyone affected by the attention economy.) A life spent pursuing people's attention would not be a Stoic way of life. In fact, the Stoic attitude towards the propagation of ideas demonstrates this in a striking purity.

Marcus Aurelius never intended his writings to be published. Indeed, at the time of his death, he expressed his wish for the manuscripts to be destroyed. It is only thanks to those people who decided to preserve his manuscripts that we can read the musings of this great emperor at all today. Posterity should thank those rebels. It is also interesting that Epictetus, another Stoic great, wrote no texts himself. His disciple Arrian wrote down his teachings in *Discourses* and *Enchiridion* (*Handbook of Epictetus*).

When it comes to Socrates, their forefather, the situation is perhaps more acute and interesting. There are no remaining texts written by Socrates himself, consistent with the idea that the famous philosopher refrained from expressing his own ideas in written form. Instead, Plato wrote about his teachings and philosophy.

It could be said that Socrates recognized the limits of the written text from the beginning. The Socratic method is based on the assumption that wisdom does not flow from a particular individual. Rather than lecturing uni-directionally, Socrates tried to enlighten others by engaging them in conversations, in which the learning was done in both directions, with him learning as well as the disciples. Socrates enlightened by enlightening others.

There is something deeply moving and democratic about the way Socrates went about conversing with people, trying to learn from them, while always aware of his own and others' limitations, yet endeavoring to come to a better understanding of the world. If that is the spirit of the Stoic attitude towards other humans, then we definitely need more of it in today's world.

I remember vividly how the Harvard professor Michael Sandel closed an episode of his famed televised lecture *Justice* by remarking that its purpose was to induce a restlessness of reason among students. When we assume that certain things are true, we tend to fall back on unthinking assumptions. This could be a dangerous habit, especially when the rise of artificial intelligence is making it likely that we will think less about things than before. It is only when we feel restless, not sure how to take a particular thing and interpret it, that we actually start to grow intellectually. That was precisely what Socrates was trying to achieve with his conversations: a restlessness of reason.

Our time is full of person-worship, and we rarely question the foundations for our admiration. In politics, it is quite typical and acceptable to endorse, admire and identify with a particular politician, whether you are living in a democracy or an authoritarian regime. People don't think it is an anachronism to talk about the charisma of a politician, even with the advent of artificial-intelligence systems and the realization that the world we live in is very complex. In popular culture, it is typical, indeed the default assumption, to think that glamour comes from a particular person. In music, we admire artists such as John Lennon, Bono, Bob Dylan, Billie Eilish and Taylor Swift so much that we make a cult of personality around them. These are incredibly talented individuals to be sure, but we are perhaps missing a whole universe of musical possibility by choosing not to see the in-betweens. Focusing too much on a few individuals might mean that we overlook others' offerings, or attribute so much glamour to these few that we do not question the quality of their work.

The predominance of a personality-centred value system is understandable – we are human, after all. It is human nature to search for the glamorous and admirable in other people and raise them up as inspirations. But we should beware of believing in any specific and fixed system of values, lest we become inflexible and lose our restlessness of reason. In addition to the cult of personality, we need to be careful about the cult of ideologies, the cult of money, the cult of fame, the cult of statistics (more on this later) and even the cult of equations, which naturally serves as the foundation for scientific endeavour, but poses the risk of losing the whole picture for humanity. On a more practical level, we must beware of being led astray by pursuing typically accepted goals in society, such as money, social status, fame, likes, views, etc. In the process of pursuing these proxy goals, we lose something valuable for our existence, the restlessness of reason, which is nothing but another way to express the fact that we are alive. And as long as we are alive, we are on a journey of transformation. Nothing is more terrible than losing the ability to transform oneself.

Also, we are living in a great time of change. The advent of generative AIs such as ChatGPT has been and is a blow to human-centred world views, in that what counts in the world of artificial intelligence is not the nature of an individual but the collective properties of groups of people. For instance, instead of treating texts written by individuals separately (which could, of course, lead to a cult of personality), generative AI systems such as ChatGPT calculate a statistical golden mean from a multitude of texts. Although the results are undeniably remarkable and of great practical use, if we stop questioning the validity of AI outputs it could easily lead to a cult of statistics – artificial-intelligence systems based on big data, where statistical reasoning is equated with truth itself. Despite its brilliance, the advent of artificial intelligence cannot be simply termed as a progress. It is potentially replacing one cult with another, and cannot be the final answer to how we humans live.

I love the idea, described in Plato's *Phaedo,* that Socrates read *Aesop's Fables* in prison. *Aesop's Fables*, in which the protagonists are portrayed as animals, have nothing to do with the cult of personality, or even the cult of humanity. They are rather keen observations of salient personality traits we find in people around us, and representations of generic human truths, with a humorous twist (in the ironic Socratic manner). In our world of generative AI, one could consider them to be statistically robust depictions of human nature. If you were to put the prompt 'compose fables featuring animals portraying some salient defects of human nature' into ChatGPT, it might well come up with storylines similar to those in Aesop's Fables (another road that leads from our time back to Socrates).

In many senses, a modern update of Stoicism would mean a revival, or renaissance, of the spirit of Socrates. But again, this should not be the revival or establishment of another cult of personality, even if that was to be a cult of Socrates, but of his approach to life.

Socrates must have been a truly unforgettable person. The way his disciple Plato writes about him, in, for example, *Symposium*, one of his greatest works, is so full of admiration and love for the philosopher. I remember reading it when I was fifteen. I was very fond of the story about how Socrates, on his way to a banquet, started to think about a philosophical question in the middle of an Athenian street, and forgot all about where he was meant to be going, so that someone needed to come and find him. But the most crucial thing here is that Socrates never intended what he said or did to be preserved for posterity. His concern was always with the here and now, and the person with whom he was conversing. Socrates was always aware of his own ignorance, mindful of the restlessness of reason and ready to embark on the journey to find truth together with his fellow person.

Do you know a person exactly like Socrates? I do. I know many. There are many people like Socrates in the world. They are generally nameless, fameless, anonymous people, working their daily jobs, never seeking attention, but full of curiosity, embracing a full love of life. They live, they love and they die. Nothing is left. They are entirely forgotten, they are never known by posterity, because they do not have a disciple like Plato. But they are certainly favourably remembered by their friends and families, because they were such good people. You must know people like this. There are many around you, once you direct your heart away from the social media craze for likes, reposts and other views of the attention economy.

If you know someone like Socrates, then you might become their Plato. If your parents are like Socrates – shy, not outgoing, never thinking of recording their thoughts for other people to read and appreciate – then perhaps you can remember them for the kind of people they are. Like Plato, you might write about them and show it to your children and grandchildren or your friends. Even if you don't go that far, perhaps you can talk about your parents, while they are still around you, and after they are gone.

By becoming someone's Plato, observing the merits and personality of that someone, you can make the world a better place, spreading the good news. When you think of life this way, you realize that there are so many hidden treasures, which make it truly rich and worth living.

Every person is like Socrates, if we learn how to see, without our eyes being blurred by proxy goals or cults of personality.

Every person is Socrates, in brilliantly anonymous ways.

That is why all roads lead to Socrates.

CHAPTER 19

Aligning with the universe

As we have explored throughout this book, humility is one of the hallmarks of Stoicism. As humans have made progress in terms of science and technology, we have, in a sense, collectively become very successful. Materially, in the modern world we are living the lives of kings, queens, emperors and empresses of ancient times. It is therefore important to keep Stoicism alive in our souls so that this success does not go to our heads. How might this be done? The crucial insight here is that humility at the human scale can be deepened, made robust and good for our mental well-being if we align ourselves with the universe.

You don't have to be a Newton, an Einstein, a Hawking or a rocket scientist to align yourself with the universe. It is just a case of using your common sense. In *Meditations*, Marcus Aurelius writes repeatedly about the futility of wishing for eternal fame. He observes that the names of people who came before him were rapidly being forgotten, and that it is only the hubris and wishful thinking of the feeble mind that assumes fame can be eternal. Within the context of our time, even the fame and glory of truly brilliant people such as William Shakespeare or Albert Einstein might not last forever. When we consider the fact that the universe we live in is expanding in an accelerating manner, we realize there will eventually be nothing around, not just people who would or wouldn't remember Shakespeare or Einstein. This kind of realization would have met with Marcus Aurelius's approval. He would not have minded the fact that one day there will be nobody to remember him either. As I have said before, everything we do is nothing but the efforts of a *medaka* fish in a pond formed by a spell of rainfall in the evening of an otherwise scorching hot land.

It is worth keeping in mind that the whole basis of Stoicism, including the idea of man's place in the cosmos, was laid before religious ideas promising eternal afterlife became predominant in the Roman Empire. So, ironically, the ancient system of thought under which Marcus Aurelius wrote is actually quite modern, and in line with the thinking of contemporary science in general, and physics and cosmology in particular. In this sense, Marcus Aurelius is our contemporary. (Actually, the ultimate accomplishment of this book, if I may so wish, would be that you are able to think, feel and live like the great Roman emperor, in alignment with the universe, humble in your success and resilient and hopeful in your difficulty, like a true Stoic. The purpose is to think like a Stoic.)

In order to be aligned with the universe, you need to open up your senses. *Grapefruit*, a wonderful book of conceptual art by Yoko Ono, contains many inspiring pieces of Stoic sensitivities. There is one which connects our everyday senses with the cosmic entities:

> Imagine one thousand suns in the
> sky at the same time.
> Let them shine for one hour.
> Then, let them gradually melt
> into the sky.
> Make one tunafish sandwich and eat.
>
> 1964 spring

This extension of one's senses to what is occurring in the universe, accompanied by an embodied feel for one's surroundings, is a trademark of Stoicism. You connect your actions to the universe through your body and feeling.

You can see this in many cultures. In Wagner's opera *Lohengrin*, there is a scene where the king proclaims that the decision in the legal court should proceed when the sun is high in the sky. This is a beautiful example of alignment of human activities with the great nature, which seems to have been one of the common senses in medieval times. In Japan, the traditional Noh play is full of references to connections with the universe, where the performer is typically seen to be making movements in a vast world, rather like a lonely space walker in spacesuit floating above the blue planet Earth. In the *Arabian Nights*, the story of the Magic Horse flying the prince off to outer space reflects the fantastic imagination of the people in the Islamic Golden Age, connecting humans with the universe. Finally, the Daoyuan ('Origins of the Tao') manuscript discovered in Mawangdui, China, tells a story about the origin of the universe that has striking similarity to our modern ideas about the big bang and gravitational singularity.

Throughout our history, we humans have always been concerned with the universe as a source of inspiration, a means to consolidate our existential status and a mirror to reflect ourselves and confirm our position. Perhaps, paradoxically, we have been assured of our own unique existence – self-consciousness is a fragile yet robust assertion of one's existence – by feeling so insignificant in face of the vast universe, a familiar experience for anyone who has looked up at the sky on a fine night . . .

No matter how important you are, how successful, wealthy, powerful, in comparison with the universe, you are nothing. The total insignificance of oneself is one of the most important elements of Stoicism.

The universe is a great equalizer. It is not that everyone is equally important, as political correctness might frame it, though that might be great for our society. It is that everyone is equally *un*important. We are all insignificant when facing the vast extension of space and time we call the universe.

In our daily lives, we can become obsessed with various proxy goals and be led astray by cults, including those of personality, ideology, money, fame and, most recently, statistics, which has led to the artificial-intelligence evo-lution. Interestingly, if the singularity of artificial intel-ligence ever arrives, people will have to acknowledge the fact that excellence does not necessarily reside within an individual, but within a network of well-connected entities, in which each of us plays but a small part. Each one of us would be just a tiny nugget in the bulk of data used to turn artificial intelligence into humanity's butterfly (see Chapter 3), to adapt the poetic phrase Geoffrey Hinton, the father of AI, used to describe the astonishing ability of artificial intelligence to come.

We might feel that we are small in the face of emerging powerful artificial-intelligent systems. This might, in fact be the spiritual emergency of our time. On the other hand, these feelings of threat induced by artificial intelligence are trivial when compared to the frightening and strangely uplifting nothingness we feel when facing the universe itself.

It is therefore interesting that the revival of Stoicism is occurring precisely at a time when the old ways of humans are potentially being superseded by the new ways of stat-istical intelligence, and the hubris of humans involved in the development and deployment of artificial intelligence is being revealed.

We need a renaissance of human values. Not as a reaction to the emerging era of artificial intelligence (that would ultimately be too shallow), but to align with the universe itself. Stoicism will be central to this new renaissance. This book has been a humble attempt to make a small ripple in that blue ocean of new possibilities for humans.

I believe that in the human soul there is something that deeply resonates with the Stoic way of living. I don't know why and how it is, but it is, apparently, the way it is.

Stoicism could well provide the new foundations for spirituality in human society.

It would be a misnomer, however, to call Stoicism a new religion of the twenty-first century. It would not be appropriate to make this venerable philosophy into a competitor of religion. It is rather that Stoicism would be able to provide a foundation for a form of human spirituality that is free from the constraints of traditional value systems, and yet aligned with modern science and our place in the universe.

In 2007, the German painter Gerhard Richter designed the stained-glass window in the south transept of the great cathedral of Cologne. It is admittedly a difficult job to design something for a place of worship today. His solution for the Cologne window was not to worship a particular person, a specific symbol or a uniquely defined building or place. Instead, his design is a painting made of various colours, in random order, in simple regular grids on a white background. I personally find this artistic creation deeply moving. It is a beautiful statement on how each individual exists in relation to others, until the colours all blend into the generic white light, coming from the source of the mother of all living things on Earth: the sun. Its abstract expression seems to suggest new ways to align our spirituality with the laws of the universe. Perhaps the journey of our spirituality has only just begun, and Stoicism is our first step.

Traditionally, the physical universe has been called the macrocosm, while the human body is the microcosm, and it has been believed there are deeply resonant analogies between them.

As a person living today, one has one's worries in the small world. The ups and downs, the joys and sorrows, surprises and the repetition of the everyday. One sometimes feels that what one does is trivial and has nothing to do with the large-scale properties of the universe. One feels so insignificant. The universe does not seem to care whether one is happy or not.

However, Stoicism shows us a way to be connected to the larger orders of the universe, and how whether we are happy or not affects the alignment of ourselves with the larger world, because we see the universe through the lens of our subjective minds. Thus, we are united with the universe, not only through the wonderful idea of cosmic consciousness but also by means of quite logical connections.

CHAPTER 20

Stoicism and you

So, our journey of Stoicism is almost over.

At the beginning of this book, I mentioned that this is an age of abundance. However, I should add here that there are fundamental limits to what humans can achieve and enjoy, materially and informationally. We need to *know* our limits. That's why we need Stoicism now.

In Chapter 7, I discussed the Promethean mindset, named after the god in Greek mythology who brought fire to humanity. At present, we Promethean humans are at liberty to decide what to do with the resources of the Earth. The human project to emigrate to Mars, with accompanying ideas of terraforming it, so that Mars' environment accommodates life, is an attempt to extend Promethean ideas beyond the Earth. Such a line of thought, although extraordinary and outrageous, is not outside the norm for tech billionaires today. But the truth is that none of us, including tech billionaires, is immune to the ecological system. Even as Promethean engineers hack incredible codes to generate next-generation artificial intelligence, inside their intestines billions of microbes are working to keep the brain–gut axis functioning. When humans plan to migrate to Mars, unless quite an extensive and representative subset of the Earth's ecosystem – a kind of contemporary Noah's ark – is brought along with them, they are unlikely to survive there. We should always remember that we are just a tiny part of the Earth's ecosystem. Promethean plans for technological and ecological growth tend to forget that.

Tech billionaires are not immune even to the ecology of start-ups. The fact is, most start-ups actually fail. But the economic system goes around as a whole, absorbing those many instances of failure into its metabolism; maybe they provide the necessary nutrients for the successful start-ups, in terms of human resources and technological learning, just like, in the ecological metabolism of the tropical rainforest, a fallen tree will typically serve as a nurse log, to help nurture young plants as a growing site. The truly successful companies, such as Google, Meta, Apple and OpenAI, are perhaps supported and nurtured by thousands of fallen ones. If you are too obsessed with the success of just one company, you tend to forget the importance of the ecosystem. You just focus on a tree and forget the forest.

The dichotomy between growth vs ecology is a major issue not only for humans as a whole, but also for humanity's route from here concerning artificial intelligence and AI alignment. We are at an important crossroads.

We need to be extremely careful from here, because we are walking on a tightrope. Nuclear weapons are still here, and humans are clever enough to make them but not wise enough to dismantle them. Game theory, which analyzes the confrontations between nuclear powers, is clever enough to put the dynamics of confrontation, based on the fear of extinction, in the mutually assured destruction (MAD) scheme, but not wise enough to tell us how not to become MAD enough to keep possessing nuclear weapons, under the ultimately unstable and unsustainable premise of nuclear deterrence. Artificial intelligence could potentially be used to solve man's many problems, cure diseases and put an end to social asymmetry and systemic injustice. Yet some are using artificial intelligence as a means for the technological arms race to secure themselves positions in the fragile ecosystem with fame and money. The hubris of the human mind, as exemplified by the Promethean attitude in the high-tech sector, might cost the human being its own existence.

Seeing all this, as I conclude this book, I do feel there is a strong case for a revival and renaissance of Stoicism. It is not just about the system, but about how we live as individuals from here, within the universe. Stoicism is a necessary piece of wisdom for humanity, not only on the individual level but also for our species as a whole. Unless we step extremely carefully from here, the survival of human civilization is not guaranteed. As we try to reclaim and revive human values at this difficult time, Stoicism is an essential tool.

So, where do we go from here? At the level of the whole human civilization, we need to be cautious about developing and employing technologies, including and particularly artificial intelligence; we need to reaffirm and reclaim human-istic values, and stoicism could play a pivotal role. At the level of individual lives, we would like to somehow cope with the difficulties of the time and muddle through from here, so each of us would be happy in our own way while respecting the unique individuality of each other. Here, again, Stoicism would play a central role. Let us not sink into technological hubris, no matter how we successful we may be in developing new technologies, including artificial intelligence. Let us align ourselves with the old Japanese adage I mentioned at the start of this book: a rice ear hangs its head low as it ripens.

Here, we return to the ten statements about Stoicism that I put at the end of the Introduction. After a journey through the significance of Stoicism, how do they read?

1. Stoicism is about how one streamlines one's resources and efforts as one goes through the uncertainties of life.
2. Stoicism is a way of making one's best effort under any circumstances.
3. Stoicism is a process by which one reappraises one's emotions to arrive at a positive and proactive view of life.

4. Stoicism is maintaining a balance of the self, body and personal agency while interacting in a complex and unpredictable environment.

5. Stoicism is coming to terms with one's own unique characteristics and traits, accepting oneself and nurturing self-love.

6. Stoicism is becoming liberated from life's proxy goals and navigating towards the heart's true desires.

7. Stoicism is aligning one's life with one's inner voices, and the laws of the world.

8. Stoicism is about seeing things clearly, knowing one's own limitations, while having a sense of wonder for the unknown and dreaming of one's eventual possibilities.

9. Stoicism is about appreciating and celebrating the diversity within oneself and in the universe.

10. Stoicism is about keeping one's personal integrity under any circumstances, so as to see clearly the shape of one's soul.

I do hope that these statements will be helpful in your life, as we go about this journey of life together, trying both to make each life, and the future of humanity, better.

Finally, I do feel that we need a Socrates among us in the world today. The Socratic spirit of being aware of one's ignorance and limits, and equipped with an inquisitive and open mind, is something we need in our society. Socrates, as the father of Stoicism, should be our guardian angel, our colleague and our companion.

The good news is that every child is like a Socrates. Indeed, every single child *is* a Socrates, with their brilliant, enthusiastic eyes and open and curious mind.

And better news still is that there is a child in every one of you, no matter how old you are. So, as I close this book, let me make a final wish.

May you align yourself with your unique personality and the universe.

May you keep your inner child alive.

May Stoicism be with you.

COPYRIGHT ACKNOWLEDGEMENTS

Every effort has been made to trace and acknowledge the original copyright holders. The author and publisher will be pleased to correct any mistakes or omissions in future editions.

The Japanese waka poem by Ariwara no Narihira on p.60 is from Episode 125, 'This Day' of *The Tales of Ise*, Penguin Classics, London, 2016. Translation © Peter Macmillan, 2016.

The haiku by Matsuo Basho on p.60 is reprinted from *The Essential Haiku: Versions of Basho, Buson and Issa* by Robert Hass (HarperCollins Publishers Inc, US, 1994; Bloodaxe Books, UK, 2013) by permission of Bloodaxe Books Ltd.

'Mirror Piece' on p.186 and 'Tunafish Sandwich Piece' on p.259 are reproduced from *Grapefruit* by Yoko Ono (© Yoko Ono 1964), by permission of Herbsman Hafer Weber & Frisch, LLP, on behalf of Yoko Ono.